THE GATHERING OF THE UNGIFTED

THE GATHERING
OF THE UNGIFTED

Toward a Dialogue on Christian Identity

JOHN C. MEAGHER

PAULIST PRESS
New York, N.Y.   Paramus, N.J.

Cover design by Morris Berman.

Library of Congress Cataloging in Publication Data
Meagher, John C.
      The gathering of the ungifted.
      1. Identification (Religion) I. Title.
BV4509.5.M4   248'.4   72-3827
ISBN 0-8091-1874-2

Contents

5

To Frank and Paul, for showing what it means to be faithed;
And to John and Helen, for two healing touches of ungiftedness;
And to the Gathering in Basil's Basement, with love.

Preface

I HAVE tried for years, unsuccessfully, to break myself of the habit of skipping prefaces until after I have read the books they were meant to precede. I keep forgetting that a preface is not only traditionally the place where the author acknowledges his indebtedness—a task for which the impatient reader, understandably, rarely shares the author's relish—but is also the place in which one may most decorously offer a few words of relevant warning or explanatory *apologia,* which is what I would like to do next.

The first matter is to solicit your patience in advance (unless you share my uncooperative habit, and have already finished the book) for a few terms and expressions that may strike you as somewhat odd—most prominently, the two key items in the title. Some of my consultants have initially found some of them a little off-putting, which makes me feel obliged to assure you, for whatever it's worth, that they were carefully chosen for serious purposes, and that they survive critical misgivings because both reflection and advice have led me to suppose that they have a good enough chance of performing the special office they were chosen for to be worth the risk of giving undesirable annoyance to some readers.

The second point is to acknowledge the regrets I have about the partial distortions and insufficiencies that inevitably arise from the condensation of arguments and ideas. If I had tackled a much longer book, some things would have been different (including, perhaps, your willingness to tackle it in turn?). There are useful distinctions to be made between faith and belief, for example; but I have not attempted to observe any such distinctions in this book, because I have here specialized in addressing myself to a common mode of understanding in which the two converge, making the potential distinctions largely irrelevant. Nor did the present business seem to me to make it pertinent to insist, as I would prefer to do, on the enduring validity of Judaism and on its critical importance to Christian theology: to represent adequately what I think on this matter would have been too much beside the main point, and I have accordingly neglected to say much that ultimately needs to be said. These and other points of refinement and qualification I hope to attend to another time; but the longer book that they would have required is not the one that I wanted to write now. Mind you, the aim of this shorter book is hardly less ambitious: I am still attempting here to meet a related set of important problems in Christian self-understanding, and what I am offering is still an exposition of the best thinking I have been able to muster about them so far. I merely want to point out that some allowances will have to be made for foreshortenings and shortcuts.

I believe that I said what I think, however, aside from refinements that I judged to be dispensable. This is the book I set out to write. I also believe, frankly, that I met the problems too; but there, of course, your judgment is more important than mine. More important even to me, since it is a better test of adequacy. As a way of preparing the book to meet that higher court of appeal, I exploited the advice of a fair number of people at various stages of writing, starting with the Rev. Myron Bloy, Jr., whose invitation to participate in a symposium on Christian Identity was the begetting occasion of the paper from which this book eventually grew. The other participants in that symposium also hacked happily away at those earlier stages of the argument, albeit with their critical talons perhaps somewhat blunted by the influence of surroundings and circumstances so memorably congenial and delightful that I hesitate to describe them lest you be consumed with envy. Just ask them: Joe Walsh, Paul Schrading, Dick Underwood, Bill McAuliffe, Sam Preus. Then I consulted friends who were kind enough not only to give suggestions here and there but even to complain about things that seemed to them to ring false until I saw that they were right and changed accordingly—Ardis Collins and Helen Nolan were especially helpful at that stage. And then, as the essay was gradually developed into the present book, I consulted Anne Adams, George Lawler, Christine Costello, Ted McGee, Marion O'Connor. There were a few others who were helpfully encouraging though less reformingly critical (including, somewhat to my surprise, my cherished and irrepressible friend Peany), but I wanted to name the ones who raised serious objections in order to establish that I gave a fair chance to get flaws pointed out. I think I made changes in virtually every instance in which a criticism was made. So if you are not totally satisfied with this book, don't blame me. I did what I could. Blame them. I'll be glad to forward your letter of complaint, if it comes to that. But I hope it doesn't. Were it not so extravagant, in fact, I could wish that reading this book might be as good an experience for you as writing it was for me.

Toronto
Epiphany, alias Twelfth Night, 1972

THE GATHERING OF THE UNGIFTED

Introduction

ONCE upon a time, says the Second Book of Kings, Israel was in very bad shape. No rain, no crops. Naturally, one wants to blame the government: and so the prophet Elijah, a one-man loyal opposition, laid the blame on King Ahab and his pagan Queen, Jezebel, saying that the root of the problem was that they had been promoting the worship of Baal in a land that was supposed to belong strictly to Yahweh, the God of Abraham and of Isaac and of Jacob. He raised hell with the people of Israel too, for fooling around with false gods, and demanded that they make up their minds once and for all: let it be Baal or Yahweh all the way, one or the other, with no compromise. How to decide? Elijah climbed to the top of Mount Carmel and built two sacrificial altars, one for Yahweh and one for Baal, and then had King Ahab gather together all the people of Israel and all the prophets of Baal. There, on the very top of Mount Carmel, Yahweh was to have it out with Baal in a final showdown—Elijah alone against all of Baal's prophets.

Baal's turn was first. His prophets prayed to him to come and take their sacrifice. All morning long they prayed and pleaded. Nothing happened. All afternoon they shouted and wailed and cut themselves up, trying to stir Baal to action. Still nothing happened—except that Elijah started baiting them and dropping a few off-color remarks about Baal himself. And when the prophets of Baal collapsed with exhaustion, Elijah gathered the people of Israel around him and prayed to Yahweh. He prayed that Yahweh show all Israel that he was their Lord and the only true God: and immediately there fell fire from heaven, and in a blaze of glory it consumed the sacrifice prepared upon the altar of Yahweh. Hallelujah!—the people of Israel all fell on their faces praising Yahweh, the only true God of Israel, and then rose and, under Elijah's direction, dutifully massacred all the prophets of Baal.

That's the Old Testament for you, you may be thinking: a happy ending every time.

Well, then. Suppose it hadn't worked out so neatly? After all, it would have served Elijah right if the Lord had declined to play his little game. What would have happened?

"*Look, Elijah,*" *said Ahab gently,* "*it's already quarter after seven. It looks like it's going to be no show. Pack it up. Try again another day.*"

"*I'll give you just fifteen minutes more,*" *said Elijah sternly, obviously not talking to Ahab.* "*Fifteen minutes. I've been pretty patient, but you know what a temper I've got when I get pushed too far.*"

"*Come* on *Elijah!*" *said Ahab testily.* "*It's getting pretty chilly here, and it will be worse by the time we get down the mountain. Jezebel has left already, she was so cold. There's nothing more going to happen here, take my word for it.*"

"*Fourteen minutes,*" *said Elijah severely, his eyes narrowed and fixed on the sky.* "*Fourteen minutes to make up your mind. I set this up in a perfectly reasonable way, and if you embarrass me and disappoint the people, you're going to have to deal with the maddest prophet in Israel. You brought our people out of Egypt, through the sea, through the desert; you gave us bread from heaven and water from the rock and the Law from Sinai; you gave us the land of Israel and a King to rule in it and prosperity to enjoy it, and now you're balking at one lousy little dose of fire from heaven!*"

"*O* really, *Elijah*,'" *said Ahab impatiently.* "*You don't really believe all that stuff, do you?*"

Elijah looked at Ahab coldly. "*You bet your ass I do,*" *he said firmly.*

Ahab looked at Elijah hesitantly. "*No,*" *he said slowly,* "*I guess I'd lose, wouldn't I? And then I wouldn't have anything to ride down the mountain. Jezebel took the horse when she left.*"

Even if nothing had happened, there would probably have been no problem as far as Elijah is concerned. He would have been enormously annoyed with the way the Lord had bungled what seemed to him to be the greatest Yahwist public relations scheme since the Exodus; but he would eventually have forgiven him, however grudgingly, and set about the more slow and uncertain business of promoting Yahweh's cause with the King and the people by the power of the word alone, unseasoned with fire from heaven. His own faith would surely have remained as sturdy as Mount Carmel.

But the King and the people themselves—that would have been a different story. How were they to recover from the confusion of such a stalemate? After all, it was on account of the shaky uncertainty of their religious identity that this affair had been set up in the first place. They came to that mountain expecting to have their spirits settled once and for all, one way or another; it probably didn't even matter much to them which way, so long as it was completely—they must have had leanings, but they were ready to go wherever the action was. What would have become of *them* if the great Either/Or of Mount Carmel had turned into a Neither/Nor?

The business of this book is to pursue the Christian equivalent of that question. It is written not to the Christian Elijahs, whose faith is clear and vivid and who need no signs from heaven to tell them who or where they are, but rather to the Christian Ahabs and the Christian Israelites, who have long since left the foothills of their unvisited Carmel and gone home. There, back among the houses and fields, where a divine intervention seems even more unlikely than on the bare mountaintop, they must find a way to come to terms with what has not happened—and to rediscover what *has*. That is what this is about.

I

"I'm getting uneasy," muttered one of the priests of Yahweh. "I mean, what if Baal really does win out? We came off lucky enough this time, but it was close. Maybe we ought to settle out of court."

"Nonsense," answered another of the priests of Yahweh. "Baal won't win out."

"But just suppose he does," said the first priest of Yahweh. "Like, just suppose."

"Don't be an idiot," snapped the second priest of Yahweh. "He won't, and that's that. Calm down."

"I wish I had your faith," sighed the first priest of Yahweh.

"Faith, hell," said the second priest of Yahweh. "Experience, you mean."

"Do you mean that Yahweh's done this before?" asked the first priest of Yahweh, excitedly.

"Not what you're thinking," said the second priest of Yahweh. "I mean he has left this sort of thing undone before. It's only in the movies that problems like this get solved by brimstone, buddy."

"Well, if it's going to be like that," grumbled the first priest of Yahweh, "then I've had it. I just can't take the suspense and indecision. I resign."

"You're stuck with it, pal," said the second priest of Yahweh. "Sure, you can get out of the priesthood; but how are you going to quit being Jewish?"

The Ungifted

WITH faith like a mustardseed, some remarkable things can happen. With maybe half a mustardseed's worth, you can probably be unshakably confident about the total truth of Christian doctrine, and utterly sure that it is exactly the answer to the world's problems, now and always. In the Good Old Days, that is where all Christians took their stand—tough, unwavering, strong in the faith.

That is no longer the way it works. True, there are still lots of Christians around who are cut out of the sturdier old fabric, who live totally committed to Christ, glowing with a certitude that seems clearly to be not of this world, rich with a spiritual gift that makes them full of power and conviction about the Faith of our Fathers. These are the Christian Elijahs, the Faithed: I salute them with reverence and pass by to the uncomfortably large number of people who form the rest of us— the Ungifted.

The Ungifted are those of us who don't seem to be measurable even in smaller fragments of the mustardseed. Far from being able to stand strong in the kind of confidence we can remember having had as children, we now find that our sense of what the world needs sometimes seems to have no more to do with Christianity than with Gothic architecture. We look into ourselves for some remnant of the faith we recall having had, and discover that about the best we can come up with now is undisbelief.

Sometimes we wonder uneasily if we are really Christians at

all. What is it that keeps the flame burning, keeps our Christianity (such as it is) alive? Certainly not what we learned long ago to call the Gift of Faith. This is something quieter and more elusive. Something less certain and less comforting, too. There is a feeling in our bones about Christianity, a pulse that still beats in our brains to its rhythm. Sometimes it seems that this is not much to go on; it's certainly a poor imitation of what we have understood since childhood to be the real thing. But this is apparently all we've got.

"When the Son of Man comes, will he find faith on the earth?" The Ungifted hear Jesus' question with a shudder of discomfort—even of guilt. Uneasy, shy in the faith, we can't promise anything stronger than loyal undisbelief. We do not wish to pretend to a faith we don't really possess, nor say that Christianity is the Answer if we don't quite see it that way. And so the Ungifted have begun to emerge into the light of day, bringing with them modified forms of Christianity, many of them compromised, watered down, waffling. We are willing to be loyal—but we want to be honest. It's not working too well, so far. Because not only are many of the compromises odd and unstable—there is also, in most of the Ungifted, the nagging guilty suspicion that the Faith of our Fathers deserves more from us, indeed *demands* more from us, whether or not we are ready to give anything more. The Faithed have not disappeared. They remain among us, bearing witness boldly to unadulterated Faith, and in their presence our ungiftedness may itself feel slightly disloyal and dishonest.

Ungiftedness is not a new problem. What is new is merely that the Ungifted are being exposed in such numbers, and dealing with their situation so publicly. They were there in earlier times too, but carefully hidden. The number of the genuinely Faithed, fully possessing—or possessed by—the Gift, was probably always small by comparison with the legions of Ungifted:

but the past had more ways of hiding the difference between them. For one thing, there used to be terrific pressures against admitting that deep down inside, one's belief was feeble or absent. To confess that would have been to risk rejection by family, friends, community—quite enough to keep one from admitting it to others. Moreover, when it was assumed that Christians were in a way *obliged* to have the gift of faith, its absence would seem to imply that one had been rejected by God—and so many were unable to admit their ungiftedness even to themselves. Besides, most Christians have lived out their lives in a basically Christian community, both local and international: surrounded by others of the same persuasion, it is relatively easy to mistake loyal assent for real belief. The child asks his elders, "What is it that we believe?" and stands by ready to accept the answer, whatever it may be, never noticing that there is something odd about being able to ask the question that way in the first place. And so, I take it, the Ungifted normally went undiscovered—even by themselves—through most of Christian history, seeming to be strong in the faith because they were loyal to its sponsors, or because they suffered in silence. Some of the Ungifted are still hidden, seeming to themselves and to others to be Faithed simply because they have never bothered to question the inheritance of Christian belief: their bold undoubt is not what we mean by the Gift of Faith either, though it often passes as a successful counterfeit, and it is not so much they whose presence makes the Ungifted feel uneasy as their rarer genuine counterparts, the true Faithed.

But even these types of hidden Ungiftedness are becoming fewer in number. Conditions have changed, and the Ungifted are brought to self-discovery. The relentless open questioning of Christianity that has always gone on among its enemies and apostates is now being more often heard and more strongly felt within the Christian fold itself. Religious disagreement is no longer a taboo subject for conversation; there is no longer, for most educated Christians, any ghetto of comfortable Christian refuge from the aggressive misgivings of a skeptical and often hostile world. After centuries of being rather otherworldly and withdrawn, Christianity has tried to meet the rest of the world face to face and has discovered that it is not as well equipped as it might once have supposed, either to convince it or to heal it. And in an age of expanded education, where at least modest critical intelligence is much more widely developed than ever before, one is expected—and one expects oneself—to take much greater intellectual responsibility for one's beliefs, to be much more cautious and tentative about holding views that one cannot successfully defend against all forms of critical investigation. No wonder that the Ungifted seem to be multiplying, and are becoming more visible: their condition is easier to discover, and less threatening to them, than ever before in Christian history.

This is not what used to be called with alarm "losing one's faith." In most cases, the Ungifted have lost nothing at all. They have merely discovered that it had only *seemed* to be faith in the first place; what had always appeared to be bone has turned out, when submitted to a pressure adequate to test it, to have been cartilege after all. The Ungifted have not lost their faith— they have found their limits.

No, what is new is not that they exist, for they have always existed, but that they are being revealed in such numbers. And what is especially new is that they are being revealed in surprisingly prominent places. Leaders of the Christian churches, from whom one might have expected to hear a reassuringly sturdy commitment to that Old-Time Religion, are now faltering along with the rest of us. It is not the foundings of new liberalized sects or the dramatic breakaways or the press-conference apostasies that form the most intriguingly significant symptoms of a new order, but rather the quiet restatements of Christian loyalty in lower and stranger keys, an uneasy tentativeness that shows that something has changed drastically. When priests and ministers plumb their own spiritual depths to discover their sources of Christian loyalty, they often find the same sort of undisbelief and respond with the same sort of gingerly groping as the rest of the Ungifted. For instance: during a recent conference of campus ministers, a college chaplain tried to describe the way in which he saw the current Christian situation on college campuses. "I think there's a theological task to be done," he said. "It has to do with vision, it has to do with the claims the numinous makes on us. We talk about those claims in a variety of ways, and for Christians, the numinous, the claim of the numinous, somehow is related to the life, death and resurrection of Jesus and the Spirit of God."

For Christians, says our spokesman, the numinous—the sense of the holy—is somehow related to Jesus and the Holy Spirit. That's our sort of ungifted creed, all right. Not that the sense of the holy is exclusively revealed to us through Jesus, or that it dwells in us through the Spirit of God; not that the numinous is the ultimate quality and meaning of Jesus and the Holy Spirit; not even that the numinous is really to be found in Jesus and the Spirit—but only that it is "somehow related." The husk of the mustardseed. Such a cautious and feeble connection between religious authenticity and the basics of Christian doctrine gives us at best a Christianity of Square One: anything less than this must surely mean the total collapse of Christian affiliation.

But anything more than this requires more confidence and faith than many Christians, including many religious leaders, can put together. There is something good and stabilizing about their loyal undisbelief. But that is not quite enough. Loyalty is neither vision nor faith, and when the Ungifted translate into their own real belief and understanding the Christianity that haunts their spirits but evades their faith, it does not look much like the traditional Christianity. A lot is lost in the translation. And seeing this, the Ungifted must face up to a painful dilemma. The Faith of our Fathers is not in fact where we live. Where then does judgment fall? Do we disqualify ourselves, or do we disqualify traditional Christianity? Or is there, just possibly, some honest and legitimate way of coming to terms with both ourselves and our religious inheritance, bridging the gap authentically?

The answers will not be the same for everyone. In some cases, self-disqualification is certainly the right solution. If, on closer inspection, I should discover that I have no interest in remaining Christian, consider the whole thing utterly opposed to the life style I want to adopt, and simply do not care whether I'm going to be eventually disappointed, disgraced or damned, then there is little sense in sticking around. Some forms of disaffection are pretty definitive. But this is no dilemma: those who decide that they want to live in a way that is incompatible with Christianity can usually make the break without discomfort. But there is another position that is quite different, and more painful: those who wonder anxiously if it is really possible to sustain both their Christianity and their honesty are often tempted to disqualify themselves, however reluctantly, on the ground that their very Ungiftedness seems to be in itself a disqualification—having lost their faith, they feel obliged to leave Christianity altogether. There is no easy solution. Such a dilemma must ultimately be met according to one's own sense of integrity. But I add only this: if your integrity supposes that ungiftedness is intrinsically un-Christian, then I say that your integrity is mistaken, and that I respectfully invite you to read on while I try to show that the Ungifted not only have a place in the multi-mansioned house of our Father, but even a fairly important place.

There are also those who, impatient with the mismatch between themselves and Christianity, stand in judgment over it and dismiss it as preposterous or dead or destructive. Let them go: they will leave painlessly and will thrive better elsewhere. Their judgment is closed and is not within the reach of counter-argument; it will not matter to them that it is not shared by even non-Christians who are reflective enough. But there is another and far more dangerously subtle way of disqualifying traditional Christianity. The Ungifted, in an act of benevolence designed to enhance the credibility of Christianity in a suspicious world, or in an act of accommodation designed to close the gap quickly between Christian tradition and their ungifted selves, are prone to "reinterpret" the tradition in a way that quietly eliminates some or all of its features and replaces them with sturdy modern materials. This hidden renovation is often well motivated, but not necessarily a happy solution. Seasoned timbers, however, creaky, are not always less well suited to the job than steel I-beams. This is no easy matter, either. One's understanding and interpretation of the Christian heritage must finally depend on the generosity and discrimination of one's own intelligence. But let me say that if your intelligence thinks that traditional Chris-tianity is no longer credible or viable, or that it doesn't much matter, then I believe that your intelligence is mistaken—and I cordially invite you to consider the reflection in the next few chapters on what is constructive and what is destructive in the Ungifted attempts to build bridges of belief and bridges of relevance between our integrity and the integrity of the Church of Jesus Christ.

II

"*I think we really ought to get together and pray over this squabble,*" *suggested the Chief Prophet of Baal.*

"*That's all right with me,*" *said Elijah.* "*Just come to the altar of Yahweh any old time, at your convenience, and I'll be glad to join you.*"

"*That would be selling out,*" *pouted the Chief Prophet of Baal.* "*Nix. We'll go to neutral ground.*"

"*Just pick your spot,*" *said Elijah.* "*You may think it's neutral ground, if that makes you comfortable, but all Israel is Yahweh's.*"

"*We have to reach some sort of agreement about the praying, too,*" *said the Chief Prophet of Baal.*

"*How do you mean?*" *asked Elijah.*

"*Some sort of compromise,*" *said the Chief Prophet of Baal.* "*So nobody will have the advantage. If we pray in Hebrew, you'll have the advantage; if we pray in Phoenecian, I will.*"

"*What do you have in mind?*" *asked Elijah.* "*I don't know Latin.*"

"*Very funny,*" *said the Chief Prophet of Baal.* "*Well, Hebrew and Phoenician are both Semitic languages. How about we just pray in Semitic?*"

"*Nice try,*" *said Elijah.* "*You would have made a good diplomat. It just happens that there isn't any such thing as Semitic.*"

"*You're a hard man to please,*" *said the Chief Prophet of Baal.*

The Tongues of Men and of Angels . . .

BUILDING bridges is a tricky and sometimes dangerous occupation. One may readily understand and forgive the would-be builder if he finally thinks better of it and decides to settle permanently on one side only and forget about ever crossing over to the other. There are two main versions of this attempt at solving the problem, one for each bank.

The one strategy consists in repudiating your ungiftedness, with all its works and pomps, and trying to pretend *as if* you had the kind of faith with which the Faithed are blessed, while being in fact without it. This is the Spiritual Retreat—a title that is meant to hover with deliberate ambiguity between two meanings: that of a purposeful meditative assembly and that of quitting the scene of the action. The Spiritual Retreat is not necessarily a cop-out or a fraud. It can be both, since it can obviously be born of a sheer incapacity to face the reality of uncomfortable tension and can take the form of a mere affectation, an impersonation of the Faithed Christian, living on this side of the gap but putting on airs about being an other-sider. But in its other sense, the Spiritual Retreat can also be a heroic act, a daring leap into the spiritual dark that trusts (or at least hopes) in a landing on the other bank—a surrendering of the ungifted self in order that a gift may have room to grow in its place. This is not merely a desperate dream: it has worked, according to the testimony of some who have tried it. There is no guarantee, since the distribution of faith is not something that we can control or compel; but if you are determined to escape ungiftedness rather than trying to find a way of living with it, and can muster the courage for such a leap of faith—whether out of faith or in faith, or toward faith, I know not, God knows—then this may be your proper way. But if you make it, remember how it was before you made the leap, and be patient and understanding if you find that not many of your ungifted brethren are able to follow your example.

The other strategy consists in repudiating traditional Christianity—on the ground that it was formed in primitive misunderstanding, or that the world has now come of age, or that God has died in the meantime—and appropriating its titles and dignities for a new form of religion, tailored to the shape of secularized ungiftedness. This, the Post-Christian Leap, can also be a cop-out, a takeover based on little more than arrogant impatience—one may think of the vineyard-workers in the parable, with their scheme to kill the owner's son, on the weird assumption that this will make them eligible to inherit the property. But it need not be so. The Post-Christian Leap is often made out of an honest admission and acceptance of the truth of one's ungifted condition. If the traditional forms of Christianity simply no longer make sense in your world, and you do not believe in the world they describe, then you must presumably begin again by making sense of where you are. This is integrity, not irreverence. All the same, it will not do as a solution to the problem of Christian ungiftedness. Ungiftedness it can handle; but nothing that winds up so radically discontinuous with the Christian past can really have the right to claim the inheritance. There are new and important forms of religious integrity on the other side of the Post-Christian Leap, but it is not appropriate to call them Christian.

In addition to these ways of doing without bridges, there are three main methods of bridging the relevance and credibility gaps that separate Christianity from the Ungifted. One seeks to preserve the traditional forms of Christianity through a trans-forming symbolic reinterpretation that takes them out of literal-ness and makes them more at home in a contemporary setting: the Christianity of As It Were. The second aims to whittle down the traditional forms to the more streamlined and efficient shape of their nearest no-nonsense contemporary equivalents: the Christianity of Brass Tacks. Still another tries to look beyond Christianity to Religion in general, and to embrace there an essential Spirit that transcends the letter.

I call this last way the Christianity of Somehow Related, after the phrase I quoted a few pages back from the college chaplain who was discussing Christianity in terms of the claims of uni-versal religious forms, in this case the claims of the *numinous*, the sense of the holy: "We talk about those claims in a variety of ways, and for Christians, the numinous, the claim of the numinous, somehow is related to the life, death and resurrection of Jesus and the Spirit of God."

In the old days, when there was scarcely any form of religion known to Christians but their own, it could easily be taken for granted that all a human being could really experience of the numinous was to be found in Christianity—fully and exclu-sively. To speak of the presence of God apart from the practice of the Christian religion was to risk seeming either silly or impious. The presence of similar notions in other religions could be variously explained away—imitation, partially shared tra-dition, demonic sabotage. But generally, there was no question but that Christianity had the only key for awakening and ful-filling all authentic religious dispositions.

We are now generally more ready to admit that there is a kind of native religious spontaneity in man that operates within various religions, producing quests and thirsts and hopes and gratitudes that have more than an accidental resemblance to one another. When our chaplain says that "We talk about these claims in a variety of ways," he presumably means that men in general experience these general religious modes, but formulate them variously according to their specific religious and cultural traditions—the Christian style of formulation being only one among many. The numinous, as the experience of the presence of a fascinating and awesome mystery, is one of these general modes, for it is attested in various religions which can hardly be claimed to have copied Christianity. But the numinous is only one of many types of experience that have led some thinkers to consider man essentially and universally religious, *homo religiosus*. The longing to be vindicated, or to experience oneself as in the right, cleared, justified, is another such: its Judeo-Christian version is usually called *righteousness,* but those traditions have no monopoly on identifying and valuing it. The need to be rescued from some peril or terror is another widespread human experience: its religious correlative is *salvation.* The experience of the unsettling and confusing darkness of ignorance and uncertainty is virtually universal, as is the religious notion of *enlightenment.* Men and religions everywhere dream of various forms of *peace* and of *purity;* throughout their struggles with isolation and division, religions carry with them various ideals of *communion,* be it with God or with nature or with other men or with all these; and through the cherished memory of privileged moments of spiritual fullness, religious men develop conceptions of *beatitude.*

These are only some of the ways in which Christianity describes its possibilities; but none of these is the exclusive possession of Christianity. All of them seem rather to be aspects of a general human religious potential in which Christianity merely participates, like the other religions. This discovery, all by itself, has been quite unsettling to many Christians, so schooled on claims for the uniqueness of Christianity that the existence of serious parallels seems extremely threatening. If

Christianity is really one of many ways to fulfill man's ultimate religious dispositions, what becomes of its *truth?* Or are we to conclude that truth doesn't matter, being itself nothing but just another cross-religious category?

Its truth is actually not jeopardized. On the contrary, this is what protects it. For how could we possibly recognize the Gospel as truly good news unless there are movements of spirit in us deeper than and prior to its message? The Faithed may be able to claim a more direct intervention, but for the Ungifted, the truth of Christianity could never be entertained, let alone acknowledged, if there were not in us a deep and universal readiness to respond to it. Therefore, if we are able to experience and evaluate religious reality at the level described by these general categories, including the reality of the Christian invitation, this should be far from unsettling: it is in fact part of the good news itself. This is the only way that Christianity could convincingly urge its truth upon the Ungifted, and the only way in which it can finally bring the salvation, peace, righteousness that it offers. That is: the fact that Christianity is congruent with the basic religious dispositions of man is the guarantee of its capacity to bless and perfect our humanity; it is one of the marks of its authenticity and one of the sources of its power. Without this, it could only be alien.

The same things, of course, may generally be said about the non-Christian religions, which make their claims and appeals on a similar ability to touch the religious essentials of human life. It is not in this that the uniqueness of Christianity lies. The other religions address themselves to the same mankind, aspire to be a way to a similar completion, respond to equivalent needs, strive to overcome universal limitations. It is therefore not at the level of potential human fulfillment that one can make a compelling case for Christianity against the others. At this level of inquiry, the claims of competing religions simply cannot be settled. There is no technique for comparing them and evaluating their differences that will permit us to conclude confidently that a religion with inspired scriptures is better for *homo religiosus* than one without, or that monotheism produces a more perfecting way of life than polytheism. Christianity, to put it simply, does not monopolize good news. Nor does it have any exclusive passport to the inner depths of religious man. It would be unreasonable to expect that it should, because it would have been unreasonable for things to have been arranged that way. No, in order to establish the authenticity of Christianity at this level—which is by no means the only level, and not necessarily even the most important one—it is quite enough to show that these underlying religious dispositions are acknowledged and respected by Christianity, and are adequately expressed and satisfied through it. It does not matter that Christianity and the basic human religious readiness are not absolutely identical.

All we can establish this way, however, is that Christianity qualifies, from a strictly humanistic point of view, as being adequate and potentially true. That is helpful in some respects, but obviously is not enough to solve the problem of the Ungifted, who remain stuck with their undisbelief. It even complicates things further. For one thing, this approach multiplies the competition, since it validates as potentially true the claims of several other religions as well as those of Christianity. For another thing, it may seem to suggest that the right way to a religious resolution is to bypass Christianity and all other individual concrete religions and deal *directly* with the numinous, righteousness, blessedness and so on. Eliminate the middleman. If Christianity is only one of several ways of getting at these basic forms of religious disposition, and at best can only manage being "somehow related" to them, why don't we forget religious differences and aim at *homo religiosus* in a way that transcends them all—and thus solve the problem of the Ungifted by graduating from the peculiarities of Christianity to the purity of Superreligion?

This sort of thing is occasionally suggested, and even sometimes attempted. On the surface, it looks rather promising. But if we push past the surface and begin reflecting on how these things work among men (however angels may worship), we readily find that the project collapses. These general categories are simply ways in which various concrete and individual religious styles resemble one another to the detached and critical eye of the scholar: they are not descriptions of the actual ways in which individual human beings experience them. The grammarian speaks about nouns and verbs, as phenomena to be found in various languages, but (whatever angelic language may be like) you and I don't communicate in "nouns" and "verbs"— we talk of consternation and ketchup, and of things that scramble and peep. Suppose, for example that I urge on you a similar kind of reform in the realm of human relations. What divides and dissatisfies us, I claim to you, is that you love her and I love him, you love this person and I love that one; and there seem to be risks and imperfections in all of them. So why don't we just recognize that he and she, this one and that one, are only alternative ways of realizing love, and concentrate on Love itself? Forget mothers and mistresses and favorite uncles: we shall transcend that kind of provincial particularity and love the human essence common to all, and thus achieve a direct and perfected universal fulfillment of the essence of humanity as Loving Man, *homo amorosus*. You reply to me, if you haven't already left the conversation shaking your head in pity, that I have lost my buttons. There is no such thing as getting at Love directly and universally. It is ourselves that need to love and be loved, not our abstract essences. Either one attends to this person and that, and learns how to love in concrete particulars, or one never makes it at all.

There is no efficient shortcut to Ideal Religion, any more than there is a way of bringing up a child speaking symbolic logic, free from the peculiarities and deficiencies of individual languages. But there is in us a sense of religious realization, a form of evaluative self-experience, by which we can know whether we are on the whole in better spiritual shape at one time than at another. We are, that is, in touch with our underground senses of holiness, enlightenment, purity and so on. Not an infallible guide, by any means, but helpful. And it is by this sort of sense that we have developed and retained a responsive feel for the way Christianity offers us what we want or need religiously. Now: if you know another religion which works better in those respects, which you are confident would be more fulfilling, more fully adequate, more capable of perfecting and enriching your life, then I suppose you are probably required in good conscience to adopt it. But otherwise, one starts again from home base. Even if religions were as indifferently equivalent to one another as languages, it remains true that we, not being angelic, can't have any language except a particular concrete one, despite all the oddities and quirks and irregular verbs that each may possess. In the long run, moreover, for even the bilingual and trilingual, the fullest and most satisfying sense is usually that which is formed in one's mother tongue, no matter how sophisticated may be one's command of other languages. That is where meaning seems somehow to be most at home. And therefore, whatever the dignity of other religions, it must be remembered that the native language of our religious spirit is Christian. However ungifted we may be, nothing to which we may or may not be Somehow Related, including angels, can quite cancel out the truth or the importance of that fact.

III

"Look," said the Chief Prophet of Baal, "we're going to have to learn to live together. What say we work out some sort of merger?"

"I don't see what sort of merger is possible," said Elijah, "unless you mean that all of you are going to merge with all of us by becoming worshippers of Yahweh."

"That's not exactly what I had in mind," said the Chief Prophet of Baal. "Look: I figure you have something of the truth and we have something of the truth; why don't we just let our differences go and both settle for what we have in common?"

"What do we have in common?" asked Elijah. "What can Baal and the true God have in common?"

"There you go again with that intolerant attitude," said the Chief Prophet of Baal. "We both sacrifice, for instance. We burn animals to Baal and get upset when people burn them to Yahweh; you burn animals to Yahweh and get upset if other people burn them to Baal. Now, suppose we just get together and burn animals, and not worry about to whom or to what."

"I don't think you get the point," said Elijah.

Sounding Brass . . .

IF there is no adequate way to solve the problem by transcending Christianity to a sphere of general religion that would be universally believable and universally relevant (that is: without any real content), then the next best thing is perhaps to subject the Christian heritage to a modern critique, and pare off what is obsolete. Get down to brass tacks.

The Christianity of Brass Tacks has been developing for a long time. It has been generations since the Christian world at large has been entirely confident of the truth of traditional Christian identity, formed in the image of Christ the living and coming Lord. But in the days of greater ecclesiastical conservatism and less freedom of expression, the misgivings were quieter—a little shuffling, equivocation, secret mental reservations on the part of the individual Christian in the face of the Church's traditional beliefs, and a tendency on the part of the Churches themselves to proclaim only the more modest claims of the Gospel. But these symptoms of ungiftedness could not stay hidden long. The mere pressure of honest integrity demanded a more open revaluation. It came, and with an unsettling strength.

The mainstream nineteenth-century form of Brass Tacks whittled Christianity into the shape of a kind of reverent goodness. The great discovery of Israel, in this view, was Ethical Monotheism; the great contribution of Jesus was that he refined and perfected it. A lovely vision, in its own way, but far too tame to be fully satisfying, and too inaccurate to stand the push of closer criticism: this simply was not the project that could fairly be ascribed to the Jesus we meet in the Gospels (nor, for that matter, was it quite what the prophets of Israel had had in mind in the first place). But it caught the fancy of the Brass Tacks mentality of the time—even in its extreme forms, which were rather like reducing the work of St. Paul to being essentially the foundation of Bible study groups. It still lingers on here and there, but for the most part was quite overthrown by the rediscovery of the more ungentlemanly and apocalyptical Jesus of the New Testament.

Then there came a new critical whittling from within the Christian fold, directed against those portions of traditional belief, including those portions of New Testament texts, that were most difficult to reconcile with what twentieth-century knowledge and habits of mind were ready to swallow. It seems fairly clear, for instance, that some of the cures reported in the Gospels were cures of what would now be diagnosed as epilepsy, others of insanity. The Gospels represent the cures as taking place through the driving out of demons. Now, we know quite a bit about epilepsy, and even a considerable amount about various forms of madness, and demonic possession just doesn't enter into our picture. Was it that antiquity had a different breed of epileptics and madmen, or rather that they had a more quaintly archaic explanation for what caused these things? And if the latter, should we not then try to give a more scientific description of what happened, rather than retaining the old mythical accounts in which cures come by the eviction of devils? Similarly, we have a rather different way of thinking about the composition of this planet from that entertained by those of New Testament times, and a different way of thinking about the spaces that surround it. We can no longer accept quite so readily the ancient and handy but quite unscientific mythic notions of heaven being in the sky and hell down under the ground. That change means that some reinterpretation is in order. If God doesn't in fact live "up there," then what is a "Voice from heaven"? Since it wouldn't really make much sense for Jesus to go up in the sky after the Resurrection, what really lies behind the account of the ascension? And what do we make of his descent into hell? These things make sense within the frameworks of ideas in which they were originally formed, but from a modern viewpoint the frameworks themselves are an unfortunate encumbrance. They are cluttered with pre-scientific mythic modes of thought which have been discredited and must be abandoned. What then do we do with the stories and ideas they have housed?

We must find a way of reinterpreting their meanings in accordance with modern ways of understanding. This is the great aim of the project of demythologizing—a necessary and creditable undertaking, without which there would have been an ever-widening gap between the ways in which Christians think about the world they live in and the ways in which the authors of the New Testament tried to make sense. That would hardly have been in the interests of Christian fidelity. Demythologizing was thus aimed at the more accurate discovery of Christian truth, rescuing the reality of Christian doctrine from the cumbersome old garments of thought which were beginning to smother it.

Not all that glitters is Brass Tacks, however; and not all that fails to glitter is lead. It is easy to blur the distinction between what modern thought has discredited and what it has merely disregarded—between the exploded myth (such as that which places heaven as a kind of land just above the clouds, or that which supposes that the world was formed in less than a week) and the merely unstylish thought-form (such as heaven-sent visions, or the concept of sin, or the performance of the miraculous). What with such blurring of distinctions and a strong release of pent-up ungifted frustrations, what began as an attempt to purge Christianity of falsifying mythical elements pushed onward toward large-scale radical reinterpretation. Having quite rightly and properly condemned those beliefs that were in fact no longer fit for human habitation, the movement pressed less legitimately farther to condemn others that merely fell below a certain (and rather arbitrary) standard of skeptical intellectual comfort. Christians were accordingly encouraged to surrender their notions not only of the omniscience and miraculous birth of Jesus, but also of his divinity, his physical resurrection, his kingdom to come. Back we went, by another route, toward Ethical Monotheism—except that this time, the reinterpreters claimed not that they were reconstructing what Jesus really taught, but that they were salvaging from his and his followers' ignorance what he *would* have taught if they had all been more enlightened. The prevailing critical habit of mind seemed to be that whatever was not quite easy on a twentieth-century predisposition would simply have to go. That was quite a bit.

The basic thrust of Brass Tacks movements is sound and important. It is a good thing for the Ungifted to discover just what their basic convictions have in common with those of the Christian tradition, so that they know where they're starting from and what sort of gap lies between the two. What is not so good is to presume that whatever lies outside the boundaries of modern ungifted understanding is incredible and false. In fact, from a detached and indifferent viewpoint, it may be argued that the boundaries themselves are just as open to doubt as the beliefs that lie beyond them. And surely to take an uncompromisingly hard-headed skeptical view of the matter is to close one's mind from the beginning. Suppose, for instance, that I come to you soaked in extensive study and reflection on human behavior and insist on taking a Brass Tacks stand on viewing human beings as radically and exclusively selfish creatures. Oh no, you urge, look at this instance of graciousness, consider that act of generosity. All self-gratification, say I: he was showing off, pleasing his vanity by appearing gracious; she has some fixation about doing "generous" things, and so that's the way she gets her kicks—some people eat chocolate, some shoot speed, some are do-gooders, but it all amounts to the same thing. We could go on like this indefinitely, but if I have decided to keep my stand until you prove an instance of *totally unselfish* behavior, you won't break me. Everything you come up with will (if it isn't simply insane) be a case of a deed which the doer somehow thought was worth doing—and no matter how generous it may be, I can always point out that there is satisfaction in doing things one believes to be worth doing, and claim that this satisfaction is the motive for which they are done. You may—and quite rightly—argue that although this motive is indeed present, there are often other motives accompanying it, many of them quite thoroughly unselfish and much stronger than the admittedly somewhat selfish gratification of acting worthily. But I can keep claiming that the selfish one is all I see, that this is enough to explain how people behave, and that you are being unrealistic and starry-eyed because you don't want to face the uncomfortable truth of human depravity.

This is of course a caricature of Brass Tacks Christianity rather than a balanced simile, but the basic pattern seems to me to be the same. It is not perverse: it is, quite on the contrary, a form of radical honesty. The Ungifted should have a clear idea of the common denominator between where they really stand and Christian tradition. The mistake comes only in the attempt to promote the Brass Tacks version as Real Christianity, as if the things that the Ungifted find hard to believe are therefore necessarily unbelievable.

Overdemythologized Christianity is fairly common now, even fashionable. Notice, for instance, the easy contempt with which a recently published verse-prayer dismisses a traditional idea while celebrating the author's favorite people, the *honest* (and presumably no-nonsense) ones:

> *I guess that people would say that I am too attached to them,*
> *Or that I should love them "in Christ"*
> *And of course, I don't love them "in Christ"*
> *I love them as they are.*
> *Don't touch a thing about them, leave them alone.*
> *I don't know what this "in Christ" bit really means.*

A mild and ordinary example. It can be paralleled easily by many stronger instances drawn from Christian writing and conversation, proposing the elimination of beliefs or even assuming that they are no longer to be taken seriously. Here and there one even finds new creeds—sometimes proposed experimentally, sometimes with more official standing within a church—whose content is scaled down to the level of general modern ungifted reservations about the traditional faith. The beliefs sketched by such creeds obviously will wear more comfortably on an ungifted mind, fit closer to the spiritual skin. But there are two quite different ways in which such a demythologized *credo* can be proposed and accepted in place of its more traditional predecessors. One is that it is taken as a minimum program for beginners in the faith, specializing in those features of traditional Christianity in which the contemporary ungifted Christian should *at least* believe. Proposed in such a way, not as alternative or substitution simply, but as basic "pass" level, shared in common by the most ungifted and the fully faithed alike, this Christianity of At Least has much to be said for it, and I shall return to it later. But when it is offered rather as Brass Tacks Christianity, the only nourishing grain that is left after we have threshed out the chaff of antique notions, it will not do.

It will not do because it begs the question. It presumes that the real deficiency lies in traditional Christianity rather than in the limitations of ungifted understanding, and that is precisely what remains to be seen. To insist that the diminished belief of Brass Tacks is really the full equivalent of traditional belief, even if the diminution is only partial, is to claim what we have no right to claim. No good purpose is served by trying to pretend that the earlier Christian Church did not believe what it thought it believed. No good purpose is served by trying to pretend that we really mean the same things if in fact we don't. And we are simply not in a position to dismiss the difference with a wave of the hand saying that it really does not matter. It has always mattered in the Christian past—has sometimes mattered to the death. It has mattered so firmly and intensely and persistently that it has left an impress on the Christian tradition which no man can decisively discredit, and which no one loyal to that tradition or wishing to belong to its modern continuation can properly ignore.

The Christianity of Brass Tacks seems obviously more credible and more relevant to the Ungifted. That is because it is formed in the image and likeness of our notions of what is relevant and credible, which in turn are formed in the image of the fashions and preoccupations of our time—which is in many ways just as provincial and biased as any other time. It seems to be a bridge for both belief and relevance, a bridge linking the Christian tradition with the integrity of modern understanding. There is a chance that this is really exactly what it is. But there is an equally plausible chance that it is actually only a stile by which we may pass comfortably and imperceptibly over the fence that separates openness from impoverishing self-deception.

IV

"*Why do you have to be so damned exclusive?*" grumbled Jezebel to Elijah. "*I mean, the royal treasury hands out quite a bundle every year for the support of Yahweh's temple. Live and let live, I always say.*"

"*There is no God but Yahweh,*" replied Elijah sternly, "*and there can be no other god worshipped in Israel.*"

"*Oh, come off it,*" said Jezebel. "*What does Yahweh care, as long as he's got first place? His temple is by far the finest temple in Israel. Isn't that enough?*"

"*No,*" replied Elijah curtly.

"*Look,*" said Jezebel, "*I suppose you think that maybe my husband can't really be king of Israel unless he wipes out all the aristocracy?*"

"*That's another matter,*" said Elijah.

"*The hell it is,*" said Jezebel. "*It's exactly the same thing. Look, I know you think that for Yahweh to be true king means suppressing all the other gods. But that's just being too literal-minded. We give him the first place, right? So in a* spiritual *way, we're doing just what you want already. Think of the* spirit *of the thing and not the letter. The whole thing is basically* symbolic."

"*Symbols work only if they command more than that,* said Elijah. "*You can't say that Yahweh reigns even symbolically unless his conditions are really met.*"

"*You're an idiot,*" snapped Jezebel. "*You are also the most naïve man in Israel. You take all that stuff so literally that you can't even see the spirit of it. It's symbolic, you meathead."*

"Wrong," said Elijah. *"The spirit is in the letter. Throw away the letter and the spirit dies."*

"What crap!" snorted Jezebel. *"You are so unbelievably out of it! After today's fiasco, I'll bet you can't find two men in Israel who believe that stuff literally."*

"Wrong again," said Elijah. *"True faith has not been withdrawn from Israel."*

"All right," said Jezebel. *"Put your money where your mouth is. I'll bet you five sheckels that you can't find two people who will refuse to worship Baal if I ask them to—at least if I offer to slip them a little consideration."*

"You're on," replied Elijah, *"and Ahab can hold the bets."*

Jezebel delivered five sheckels to Ahab; Elijah bent down, wrote on a piece of leather, and handed it to Ahab.

"What the hell is this?" asked Jezebel, grabbing the piece of leather from her husband.

"My I.O.U.," said Elijah.

"Wait a minute," said Jezebel angrily, *"it isn't even signed!"*

"That doesn't matter," said Elijah. *"It still symbolizes five sheckels."*

"Not in the courts, it doesn't," snarled Jezebel. *"You put your signature on this, buster, or it isn't worth the hide it's written on."*

"I think," remarked Elijah, *"that you're beginning to catch on."*

. . . and Tinkling Symbols

THERE is still another way of potential bridging left. If we cannot find an authentic equivalent in a more expansive order of
religious reality, nor in a diminished order, there is still the possibility that we may take the traditional content of Christian self-
understanding as it is, but relate to it differently. Suppose we
can get around the stark either/or of true and false, and find a
kind of "true-in-a-way" through which we can relate to the
Christian basics? Just such a possibility has been increasingly
opened to modern understanding through the development of
our grasp of symbolism. The symbol cannot be impaled on the
simple yes and no by which other forms of truth are filtered; it
has an elusive truth that could turn out to be precisely the sort
of truth that ought to be attributed to Christian doctrine, the
sort of truth that it has really possessed all along, even though
it could not be clearly understood that way until now.

There are important developments within traditional Christianity that appear to invite this approach. Generation after generation of Christian thinkers have meditated on what they took
to be the content of the faith, and from their meditations have
come a rich collection of discoveries and insights. In many cases,
the derived insights are much more spiritually central than the
original doctrine. For instance: the story of Adam and Eve has
been interpreted to emphasize that all men are brothers, and
that they carry within them the possibility of a nearly divine
perfection. Now, once those discoveries have been made, they
can be held to be true quite independently of whether Adam and

Eve are to be taken literally. One can defend the notions of brotherhood and human dignity on other grounds. Our "first parents" thus become symbolic, a poetic point of convergence for more important ideas—a "true-in-a-way" whose real substance consists in its being the imagination's gathering place for various more interesting and inspiring truths. If we can give up the literalness of Adam and Eve while still keeping them meaningful as symbols for the ideas of human brotherhood and man's divine image, we have surely saved the better part and lost little. Is this the right road for the Ungifted to travel?

No one who has done much thinking about it would be likely to deny that the symbolic dimension of reality is of enormous importance in determining how we relate to the world. Even the most real, solid, historical events become "meaningful" for us only to the extent that they acquire a symbolic resonance and thus get lifted out of their confined historical moments and into relevant relationship with other times and places. The moments of my own past that are for me the most significant are not moments that have a built-in claim on me later, like the moment in which I put my signature on a contract: they are rather happenings which bind me in no way, but which I want to keep alive because they can stay valuable, either as blessings or as warnings. The only thing that keeps them from being simply dead, vanished, no-longer-real, is that I accept them not just as having happened but as *meaning* something, with a meaning that outlives and outreaches the moments themselves. Their historical lifespan has long since ended, but I preserve their meaning in memory, and choose to continue to belong to it and to have it belong to me. And so it is with all meaningful events. What claim can be made on me by the Alamo, or the fires of Auschwitz, or the moon landing, if I choose to resist? These are none of my doing, and are no longer present in living time. They can matter to me, and enter into the ways in which I form and guide my life, only if I accept them as meaning for me something which they have no power to impose merely by virtue of their having once been real. Unless I take them as representative of a human courage or brutality or accomplishment in which I can or do participate, they are as unmemorable as your thirteenth date or your last haircut. It is not the fact that it happened but what it means that finally counts, and its meaning depends in part on what I will let it mean.

Not only is history dependent on becoming symbolic before it can exert much influence: the purely symbolic can be effective even without being at all historical. There doesn't have to be a real and historical Uncle Sam for that figure to be tellingly used to organize the characteristic homely warm patriotism with which he is associated: and there doesn't have to have been a real and historical prototype of the Prodigal Son for me to draw from his story all the hope and inspiration intended by its original teller. Historicity, in cases like these, would be at best an interesting coincidence: it would add nothing to the effectiveness or relevance of that imagined symbolic non-historical figure.

One of the important developments in religiousness over the last few generations has been a movement developing out of this kind of realization, in which we are invited to accept the symbolic side of religious fundamentals quite apart from whatever historical value they may or may not have. Thus it may be argued that the Israelites need not really have been chosen by God, or led through the sea safe from Pharaoh's pursuing armies, or given the holy Law at Sinai: what counts is rather the symbolic values that got attached to these ideas—a people's sense of great dignity and destiny, its grateful understanding of its dependence on a benevolent God, its deep reverence for the importance and value of its legal traditions and religious customs. Thus detached from historical moments, these symbolic values become more generally relevant, more widely available to the rest of mankind; for if the Chosen People is a real and historical group of Israelite tribes, then they are in and we are out—but if "Chosen People" is rather a purely symbolic notion, then you can belong if you fit the meaning. Whatever your historical relationship to Israel, all you need is to think of yourself as being in some poetic sense "chosen by God," and you can be as privileged as Moses. The same techniques can also be applied to Christian fundamentals. The crucifixion can be understood as a saving historical event, but it can also be taken simply as a symbol of the thoroughness of Jesus' love; or, taking it further away from the flatly historical, it can be accepted as a dramatic reminder of the need for us to be ready to sacrifice everything for the will of God; or, at a still greater remove, it can be taken as simply another version of the parable of the grain of wheat, expressing the need for us to let go of ourselves in order to be adequately open to the truth: and it need not have been acted out in history to have that meaning. And so on—all the way to what must (I hope!) be the ultimate vulgarization: "the cross is a plus sign."

Such a search for the fullness of meaning that may lie within the symbolic dimensions of Christian doctrines is obviously a worthy endeavor. It can be carried out with tact and skill, so that in concentrating on the ways in which the various meanings are related to us, one never loses track of how they are related to each other and to the historical truths on which they are founded. Done that way, it is an enrichment of one's meditative understanding and one's sense of the relevance of traditional doctrine. But in fact, it doesn't tend to work out so well. Especially in our time. Feeling progressively uneasy about the awkward basic Christian doctrines themselves, and having easy access to a rich inherited body of symbolic overtones discovered in them by centuries of thoughtful reflection, we tend to ignore or discount the former almost entirely and concentrate exclusively on the latter. ("Creator of heaven and earth? How could that possibly square with what science tells us! But it's a way of speaking of the greatness of God anyway. And born of the Virgin Mary?—that seems too fairy-taleish, but it does serve as a reminder of how uniquely important Jesus was . . .") And by gradual degrees, it has proved easy to slip into a habit of emptying these things of literal and historical content and inflating them with meanings of a more rarified and personally congenial kind, until they all float prettily in the skies of our minds, lovely, tidy, and safe. The cross is a plus sign.

One need not go that far, of course; but there is a strong tendency to do so. Purified meaning is pleasurable; aesthetic relevance is the easiest kind to live with. Often, the more aesthetic distance we can get from things, the more beautifully meaningful they can become. The modern suburbanite hangs decoratively in his living room the huge kettle which his great-grandmother cursed as she burned her arm while boiling diapers; the tourist, who locks his car doors and hurries through the rougher part of his own town, brings back from his trip exquisite slides of picturesque European slums, touchingly poignant reminders of how the other half lives. The more we can manage the meanings of things, the more comfortable we can be with them, the more easily and thoroughly we can get out of their clutches and onto safer and higher ground from which we can enjoy relating warmly to what might otherwise be challenging, threatening, terrifying. Fallen humanity often prefers cosmetic cover-up to painful cure. And in just such a way many now deal with Christian belief, preserving its content—carefully eviscerated of its weight and vitality—ornamentally in the rooms of their minds, quaint and homely intellectual antiques that gain in meaningful charm by being taken out of active service and refinished to suit the rest of the furniture.

The symbolic dimension of Christian truths is the way they

exercise their relevance. But there are two different ways of entertaining symbols. The way I have just described is a way of entertaining their meaning without accepting their authority. That is the neatest way of assassinating a symbol, and can be quite effective. For what really counts in the symbolic dimension of doctrine is precisely what is eliminated by that approach. What matters is not that they be "meaningful" but that we be submitted to them—not their suggestiveness but their rights over us. There is an old war poster that has recently been resurrected as a decorative item: a stern and serious Uncle Sam pointing straight out of the picture, with the caption "Uncle Sam Wants *You*." If you view this as a forty-year-old in a museum or a friend's recreation room, slightly tweaked by nostalgic recollections of those to whom it formerly pointed, you miss its authority altogether. It is made to be seen by a twenty-year-old in the street, knowing that it is pointing to *him,* calling to *him,* making a claim on *him.* And so it is with central religious symbols. They are not simply "meaningful," they are imperious. If we rob them of their authority and aggressiveness, we should not deceive ourselves into supposing that we have really kept the symbols. We have kept only their husks.

I do not think it too exaggerated to say that the whole history of Christian failure has been essentially the story of people's failure to permit key symbols to make rightful claims on them. ("Yes, God has adopted you among his sons—but that needn't cramp your style." "Sure, I realize that this irresponsible baboon is my brother in Christ, and if he doesn't pay every last fraternal cent by the 15th, I'm seeing a lawyer." "Right, Christ died for their sins too, and now we're going to make sure that *they* do.") Christians have always managed to keep them meaningful—and indeed often became the more emphatic about their meaningfulness the more their authority was dodged and affronted. A purely "meaningful" Christianity is only a Christianity of As It Were, and is effectively dead—for the meaning killeth; the authority giveth life.

So if Christian doctrines are symbolic, they cannot be symbolic only at the level of As It Were. They begin to make a difference only when they are treated not as "sort of like" realities, but quite simply as realities. If in my heart of hearts I resolve: "I will behave toward her as if she deserved to be treated as my equal," I am not likely to make it: my conviction already presumes that she does not really deserve this, that she is not yet really my equal—and how shall I ever manage to live in accordance with what I actually take to be an unreal pretense? No, I must go farther if I am really to advance at all. I must resolve to live not in such a manner as to make us *seem* equal, but in such a way as to make us *be* equal. Anything short of this has doomed itself to failure. Similarly, the proper relationship of a Christian to Christian doctrine is not to regard it as richly meaningful, or even as virtually true—but as true. No compromise, no squirming: submission. Anything less will murder an important part of what it can mean.

This is the way it works not only with the factually or historically founded symbols, such as the Resurrection, or the Creation, but even with those that seem to be purely symbolic without historical content. To have life, a symbol must be rooted in living history: if it is not eligible for its own, then it must have mine. Even the Prodigal Son, fictional though he may be, must finally be submitted to if he is to be fairly dealt with. On the one hand, he must be allowed to communicate a conviction about God's forgiveness—not about how it would be nice if God worked, or about how we needn't feel sinful or guilty about what we've done, but about how God really forgives. And on the other hand, he must be allowed to point his finger not at the children of a vanished generation or at the sidewalks of another place and time, but squarely at me, now, with a command and an invitation that really apply. In the long run, any symbol that does not make this claim on my life, anchoring its meaning in the bedrock of my real historical world, is nothing but a spook to tease my mind. If it does not secure that foundation, it can never be adequate to my life.

This may seem to imply that the only history or factuality that finally counts is really mine, after all, and not that of the symbol—that I am free to dispense with a sense of the historically literal, the factual, in the rest of religious symbolism provided that I am careful to let the poetry of doctrine move me effectively and influence my life. This is perhaps the most subtle dodge of all. There is a lot to be said for it, in fact. Fictional symbols have indeed an enormous power to inspire and guide, without our supposing for a moment that they are other than fictional. Alexander the Great took his copies of Homer's poetry with him on campaigns, and there can be little doubt that he was strengthened and encouraged significantly by the influence of Achilles and Hector and resourceful Odysseus, probably more than by any historical warrior. The outrages depicted in *Uncle Tom's Cabin* stirred more people against slavery than all the real and historical sufferings of slaves put together. Hundreds of thousands of people have reformed their lives in accordance with the gospels of Young Werther, Pollyanna, Peter Pan. No one can possibly doubt the great effectiveness of the purely poetic symbol in transforming the imaginations, and the lives, of real people. Can it not be the same with traditional religious doctrine? May it not remain just as effective if accepted as having the kind of truth which poetry has—as a *purely* symbolic representation?

It may be that some people's heads are put together in that kind of way, but I think not most. Perhaps not even many. Let me give an example:

I found out recently that a friend of mine had an audience

with Pope John XXIII just before the Second Vatican Council opened. He had been to the Vatican before, in calmer times, and was struck by all the increased personnel he saw around. So he asked the Pope: "How many people are working here now?" "Oh, about half of them," replied His Holiness.

A delightful story, I think. But when I say that I recently "found this out," I mean only that I was told it—not that I have managed to verify it. In fact, since I heard this version, I've come across another one, told this time (with the necessary adjustments) about Calvin Coolidge. I rather like the Pope John version better, but when I return to it after the other, something has happened to it. Naïvely, I had taken my friend's account as factual. He was simply giving a better setting to the story, knowing that this apparent grounding in history would make it funnier. Now that I know that, it just isn't as amusing as it had been before. It is still, in a way, "true," to the extent that the late lamented Pope was that sort of person (and the Vatican's rate of efficiency probably just as eligible for that sort of innuendo as that of Coolidge's White House, or any other large operation). But if it is not grass-roots true, literal and historical and not just an appropriate kind of as-it-were, it loses something. What my sense of humor longs to find embodied in human life must remain relatively unsatisfied if this is cleverly made up at the leisure of some wag rather than, as it first seemed, the spontaneous eruption of some great leader's deft impromptu wit. It's a good story one way or the other; but if it had really happened that way, it would have been better, and would have proved more.

For despite the power of the purely symbolic, the fictional, the frankly as-it-were, there is a deep human bias for the literally and historically real, and nothing symbolic can be fully satisfying unless it goes all the way. No matter how lofty one's poetry may be, one cannot in the long run remain entirely indifferent to the vulgarity of fact. We do care. The Unknown Soldier is not significant as an individual, but as a symbolic presence that stands for all those whom the wars have destroyed; but it matters that there is a real unidentified soldier buried there, in that very place, to serve as the anchoring truth of that symbolic presence—without this, it would still be a symbolic monument, but the experience of it simply wouldn't be the same. Collectors pay vastly more for originals than for nearly perfect facsimiles; tourists put up with hours of inconvenience just to get to the very spot—homely though it may be—where the great event really took place or the great man was actually born; real tears of nostalgia are shed on the precise day of the anniversary (and real tears of disappointment if another happens to be a day or two late in remembering).

One may complain that this bias toward the concrete, the historically factual, the literally true, is a regrettable superstition that causes a great deal of unnecessary inconvenience and distorted evaluation. Why should one day be considered significantly different from another, just because of what once happened at a certain point in the earth's orbit? Why should we suppose that anything of the vanished past still clings to the places where it happened, or that it matters in the slightest whose hands touched or signed or formed this object? There would indeed be a certain gain in convenience if one could be entirely detached from such literalism, and it may well be possible that with careful training, one could arrive at a state of understanding in which symbolic values and resonances became altogether independent of factuality, and could be usefully deployed *ad lib*. Why not?

I occasionally suspect that this may be the most important question to be faced by twentieth-century power over social psychology—with all its successful achievements in the effective use of artificial "atmosphere," manufactured glamor, contrived images, canned laughter. We could probably cease to care, if only by losing track of the difference in the midst of so many purchased claims to instant history and synthetic success. Why not?

As far as I can see, the main reason for resisting is that it would, for all its advantages, cost something irreplaceable. To cut meaning loose from factuality does result in greater flexibility in the distribution of meaning, but it impoverishes the meanings themselves. If we did this, nothing could again be quite as delightful as it would have been if Pope John had really said, "Oh, about half of them." The world would go partly stale: the treasured keepsake would degenerate into an Old Thing, the place where it really happened could mean no more than Anyplace, the joyful day would surrender its claim to joy. And with the loss of those deeper, more thorough, more solid and intractable spots of meaning that now landmark our lives, the *real* would become the "real," more manageable and convenient but pale and thin. For all its potential efficiency and convenience, that is not, thank you, where I want to live.

We have some control over meanings, but we may not allow ourselves to make free with them altogether. The invigorating thrill of a dramatic encounter is real and meaningful all by itself—but if I cease to care whether anyone was hurt by it, or whether I was really alert enough at the time to tell real discovery from superficial excitement, then I am self-betrayed. Meanings must grow out of the meeting between human awareness and what really happened; they are not to be imposed against the grain of fact, or in contempt of the full truth. If we lose track of this, if the relationship of meaning to history stops mattering to us, we ourselves become partially unreal.

And that is why I think that despite the considerable human genius for valuing and responding to symbols that are not literally or historically true, no version of the Christianity of As It

59

Were can finally be adequate. No meaning or "truth" can be fully authoritative—and thus not even ultimately meaningful or true—if its symbolic vehicle is not firmly parked on the bedrock reality of history and fact: for as long as we continue to experience ourselves as historically real and imbedded in a world of vividly unique things and happenings, no religious symbol can make firm claims on us, or even reach us entirely, without sharing in that homely factuality. We don't really have our cake until we eat it: if Christianity is not *really true,* then there is no way that it can be sufficient.

Where does that leave the Ungifted? Stranded: for if detached symbolic senses can provide no refuge from the inadequacy of undisbelief, we are back where we started. The basic character of ungiftedness is, after all, precisely the inability to know with thorough conviction that Christianity is really true. And if anything, this impasse further complicates even the problem of relevance, rather than alleviating it, since its main implications suggest that basic Christian doctrine is indeed *at least* as remote from where the action is as it may have seemed before we tried bridging the gaps with interpretations that made the creed a code for contemporary preoccupations.

It is an advantage, though, to have the terrain cleared of false shelters. At least we know where we stand, and what won't do. The Ungifted are not so easily rescued. They stand within—or is it only before?—a Christianity in which they do not really believe, and whose relevance to their lives and values is questionable. Is there any way for such a one to be authentically and honestly Christian? Is there any good reason for him to bother trying?

V

"No," said Elijah firmly, "I've never had a moment's doubt."

"Well," sighed Ahab, "I suppose that's one of the advantages of being a prophet. Being a king is a little different. I mean, you have to keep on your guard. You have to be a little suspicious of everybody and everything. You get in the habit of not being able to take anybody's word for it completely."

"You have to," said Elijah, even more firmly. "You have to believe these things completely."

"That's all very well to say, Elijah," pouted Ahab. "In fact every member of my cabinet says that about every report he gives me. Can you imagine the shape this country would be in if I believed everything I was told I ought to?"

"This is different," said Elijah. "This is the Truth."

"That's what they all say next," said Ahab. "It never fails."

"But this is the word of the Lord," said Elijah sternly.

"Right," said Ahab languidly, "the Assyrian ambassador tried pulling that one on me just the other day. Usually they don't go that far, but we got into this sticky disagreement about paying that annual tribute, and he finally stood up solemnly and, so help me, that's what he said, word for word. 'This is the word of the Lord.' It was quite a performance."

"You know my stand on paying any tribute to Assyria," growled Elijah. "If the Assyrian ambassador said it was the word of the Lord, then he was lying."

"Funny you should mention," mused Ahab. "That's exactly what he said about you."

The Baltimore Cataclysm; or the
Westminster Confusion

THERE is no evading the judgment of the cumulative experience of the Christian Church over nearly two thousand years: the true believer is the Christian who is confident of the truth of Christianity, and that matters enormously. If we are to talk about the content of Christian belief, or about what Christianity teaches, it would be illegitimate not to begin with what has been over the centuries the consensus of the Christian Elijahs—those fully gifted with faith. That consensus is more or less embodied in the early creeds, which attempted to sum up that which was basic to belief from the time of the apostles, and which have stood as objectifications of the faith, the Constitution of the Believing Church, for some fifteen centuries.

From the beginning, and still in our own time, there have apparently always been Christians whose solidity and wholeness of faith would not leave room for the least razor-edge of irony or doubt. There have always been the pseudo-Faithed too, the merely unthinking promoters of a Christian party-line; but they are not to be confused with the authentically Faithed—and it is the latter who exemplify what Christian faith finally means, just as it is and always was the "saint" who embodied the norm of Christian love.

Not many have that kind of sanctity. Most of us shuffle along in a rather low-grade way, loving a little here and there but hardly having an idea of what it would be like really to become what we are called to be. Similarly, when it comes to faith, many are called but few are chosen. The Ungifted have a vague idea of what it would be like really to believe, but we peer at such a vision over a large gap. Is it a bridgeable one?

It undoubtedly feels wider, and more unbridgeable, now than ever before in the history of Christianity. Difficulties and unsolved problems that could be ignored in the days when virtually everyone in Western society was Christian seem much more uncomfortable and bothersome, much more destructive of confidence, now that the West has generated a substantial detached and critical post-Christian contingent—rather like the way you started feeling about your car after Ralph Nader showed up. A closer look at other religions has sharply changed the old assumptions about how unique Christianity is, which has disturbed still further the popular assurance of its truth. These are sobering factors, and they deserve to make a difference. But a considerable part of the feeling of unbridgeableness is a situational illusion, an exaggeration that comes from two peculiar features of this moment in time: one is where Christian self-understanding has just recently come from, and the other is what has just recently happened to understanding in the surrounding general culture.

By "just recently," I mean over the last few centuries, but especially over the last generation. Things happen rather slowly within a large body of human beings, and transformations of understanding have peculiar time-rhythms. Most of us are by now quite clear about whether the earth orbits around the sun or vice versa, and realize that insanity is not to be reduced to demonic possession and/or lack of moral restraint—and even fairly recent realizations, such as the virtues of penicillin, are widely known. But some old discoveries still haven't completely sunk in, and some old rumors still keep their unfounded hold on people's minds: hotel builders must still bear in mind that significant numbers of prospective guests have not yet grasped that the safety of the thirteenth floor is not statistically unlike that of the twelfth and fourteenth; each new generation of children continues to learn from somebody that ostriches stick their heads in the sand to hide, and that you can get warts from handling toads; and although hardly any informed person since the time of Queen Elizabeth the First has had any doubt that Shakespeare wrote Shakespeare's plays, the less informed continue to this day to entertain the arbitrary and groundless suspicion that it was maybe somebody else.

Thus although some discoveries and changes of view manage to become general (and sometimes nearly universal) cultural property in a relatively short time, others remain confined to small circles of people for centuries—and then sometimes suddenly deluge a large part of the rest of the people with the abruptness and impact of real news. This is all the easier if one group tends to be sealed off from another—the medical researchers don't talk to the witch doctors, and thus don't find out that there are a few really important and effective remedies they have been brewing for centuries; the man in the pew doesn't talk to the biblical scholar, and thus doesn't find out that it has been realized for hundreds of years that there is no good reason to think that Paul wrote the Epistle to the Hebrews; the Protestants don't talk to the Catholics and thus, generation after generation, don't find out that "saint worship" isn't really what it is sometimes cracked up to be, or reveal that "private interpretation" is not as whimsical or uncontrolled as may sometimes be suspected. Then, suddenly, someone pulls the plug or drops the barrier, and the "news" rushes in, and with the force of a long-gathered wave finally breaking, carries away with it the debris of battered assumptions and broken attitudes.

A lot of this sort of shock-wave discovery has taken place within the more conservative Christian churches over the last generation or so. The fundamentalist notion of the literalness of the Bible's truth has taken abrupt setbacks in some parts of the population; in others, the less conservative idea that there are no errors of fact in the Bible has suddenly buckled under pressure. Educated Catholicism about a generation ago generally presumed that Catholic apologetics was sufficiently well-developed and airtight that any reasonable man of good will in cooperative open dialogue with a trained Catholic scholar could be logically led to acknowledge that the Catholic Church has the only true religion. Now it is more generally recognized that things aren't quite so logically clear—that even the traditional proofs for the existence of God are not necessarily convincing to every intelligent and consistent mind. And during the same generation, the Catholic faithful have witnessed disciplinary and doctrinal controversy at high levels (where things used to seem unanimous) and have gone from what was a virtually total and unquestioning trust in the rightness of papal guidance to a startlingly huge movement of ecclesiastical disobedience and widespread misgivings about the intrinsic soundness and authority of the Pope's teachings. Unsettling.

There have been some developments which have enhanced the confidence of Christians in their tradition. For instance, the scholarly tendency in the first half of the century, which fostered the view that the early Church had disregarded the teaching of Jesus and substituted one of its own, is now being met by a counter-tendency which emphasizes the continuity between the two. But on the whole, the effect of the recent transformation of understanding and attitude has generally been demoralizing. Catholics now have had their smugness undermined vis-à-vis Protestants, and can no longer assume that if they *really* understood they would join the Catholic Church; and they have had their security damaged internally, with the breakdown of unifying discipline and the unsettling of the traditional presumption that The Church Always Knows. Christians generally have been shaken up by the conclusions of biblical scholarship, intimidated by the views of modern science, and made anxious by the disaffection and hostility of a largely post-Christian environment. All these phenomena have appeared before, and are not in that sense new. But they used to come in doses small enough that they and their effects could be absorbed fruitfully, like the modest-sized germ culture that vaccinates. What is new is merely that Christianity has recently had to take such a big dose, affecting more Christians more abruptly and in a shorter time, and is now experiencing the resultant shock.

For all the discomforts in this abrupt shaking of security, nothing in it is fatal to basic Christian claims. Indeed, it is a pity that more of it didn't occur much earlier (and in at least some cases it might have been faced and sufficiently absorbed centuries ago, if Christian leadership had been more discriminating and less protective). But it all *feels* rather crippling, even if it actually isn't, because we haven't yet had enough time to get used to the loss of so many illusions of security that we had been carelessly relying on. All the process really amounts to is that Christianity, rather belatedly, is putting away the things of a child. High time. But for a while, the feeling is inevitably shaky, the confidence in what remains is inevitably damaged, and the Ungifted above all may wonder if there is any way of supposing Christianity to be credible any more. When you first find out that there isn't really a Santa Claus, you may be pardoned if for a while you have serious doubts about the existence of Daniel Boone, Charlemagne, Knute Rockne, and that uncle in North Dakota whom various members of your devious family claim to have met.

What Christianity has had to face is that not to be Christian is neither silly nor ignorant, neither vicious nor ungenerous. It amounts to little more than that, though it seems worse. It is hard for the old-fashioned aristocrat to wake into a world of hard-headed democracy and discover that nobody else considers him entitled to his old accustomed rights and privileges. When that happens, though, the days of wine and roses are definitely over: and from now on, he can afford only a more modest conception of himself, a more humble life-style, even if in fact his new humility makes him even more worthy of respect than ever. It is this kind of thing, not worse, that has befallen Christianity —having been incautious about its pretenses to various unearned forms of authority in the past, it has been divested of them and put in its place. That's not so bad. Or novel. Over the years, it has happened to philosophy, royalty, parents, and male chauvinists—and although it is at first uncomfortable to undergo the humiliation of "friend, go down lower," in the long run, one's place is where one ought to be put. If the Christian nation once thought itself destined to conquer the world, and now thinks of itself rather as being the place to which everybody ought finally to emigrate, the place where all men may at last feel most at home, I call that an advance in self-understanding, not a loss, no matter how uncomfortable it may be when one first learns to abandon imperialistic dreams.

Part of present Christian insecurity, then, is merely the result of having so recently grown out of some long-cherished illusions. But there is another important source of insecurity—and a much more subtle and hidden one—found in the general world in which modern Christianity is embedded. And that is this: there are prejudices built into the way in which the modern world prefers to understand reality. If one is loyal to these prejudices, and views the world through them, Christianity is put at a disadvantage and tends to appear quaint, a little bit fantastic— incompatible with a seriously realistic view. This bias is implanted so deeply in us and in our culture that it usually goes quite unnoticed and unrealized. As is the case with accents, the world-view which one grew up into seems so basic and normal, and all others seem so evidently odd and distorted, that it is difficult to think of one's own native view (or tongue) as a bias (or accent) at all. But so it is. And as an illustration of how deeply and strangely it accentuates our thinking, let me ask you this: what flower would you ordinarily think of as being especially associated with beauty and romance?

Now, if you have a dictionary at all handy, try looking it up. I take up the one which happens to be by my side (it doesn't much matter which one it is: I have checked several of them on this kind of question in the past without finding any significant differences), and this is what I find under "rose": "1. any of the wild or cultivated, usually prickly-stemmed, showy-flowered shrubs constituting the genus *Rosa*, having in the wild state a corolla of five roundish petals. 2. any of various related or similar plants. 3. the flower of any such shrub, of a red, pink, white, or yellow color, and often fragrant."

I think the odds are pretty strong that you chose the same flower for beauty and romance. But in any event, no one who has much acquaintance with Western culture would be likely to be unaware that the rose has a highly romantic image in our tradition. When it comes to the meaning of *rose*—whether the word or the flower itself—there is no denying that the romantic element plays an extremely important part. In fact, *rose* probably exerts about three-quarters of its influence between being romantic and being beautiful, and the word "rose" means, in the history of its use in English, primarily "that well-known romantic and beautiful flower."

But where in our dictionary article do we find the least shadow of these truths? They are not honored. They are not even acknowledged. Pity the poor Eskimo who, armed with this dictionary, tries to figure out the point of some English poet's standard and hackneyed comparison of his mistress to a rose. (The lady is prickly-stemmed, maybe? Or has a showy corolla?)

68

Now, why would a dictionary, which takes upon itself the responsibility of recording what we really mean by our words, be so strangely careless as to omit the most important ranges of meaning behind this word? The answer to that question is basically the same as the answer to this one: why have you always thought of dictionaries and encyclopedias (which behave pretty much the same way) as being sound and adequate registers of meaning, when they are constantly playing tricks like this on us? The answer to both, that is, is that in the last analysis our sense of the really real is strongly biased in favor of the ways in which scientists and historians objectify things—indeed, biased in favor of the most naïve forms of science and history, putting almost all the premium on empirical, provable, brute *fact,* as if nothing else really amounts to anything when the chips are down. It's not only roses that suffer as a result. People have problems, too. My dictionary also has a biographical section, where I find, opening at random, that "Rainer Maria Rilke, 1875–1926," is a "German poet and author, born in Prague." What the devil does it matter where and when he was *born?* He didn't become very interesting until several years later, by which time he was circulating internationally, especially around Paris, Venice, and Switzerland, his birthplace having had about as much influence on him as his obstetrician. What sort of poet? What kind of author? Minor or major? A German Ogden Nash? A Prague-spawned Robert Service? No help. (Just for fun, I go off to check a huge unabridged dictionary, and am told: "Rainer Maria Rilke: 1875–1926. *Austrian* poet, born in Prague"!—italics and bemusement mine.)

The point of all this is not to suggest that dictionaries cheat us in their portrayal of the meaningful realities with which they deal. It is rather that the dictionary may be used as a mirror in which we may see how we cheat ourselves in our impoverished notion of the really real. For the dictionary only reminds us of the way our own critical bad habits betray what, in freer moments, we ourselves tend to think. The sturdy facts which here pose as the true meaning (setting aside the problem of whether the information is really sturdily factual) are symptoms of a sad, and perhaps tragic, prejudice on the part of the mind of our time. It is surely fair to say that these are basic features of the reality of the things in question: as I suggested before, they form a kind of bedrock of the real. But that does not mean that they are the main or key features: they are an indispensable substrate, but are to the full meaning of these realities as the bedrock is to the finished building that is built upon it. There is some sense in having a prison record or a draft card identify a given person by the mole on his cheek, the scar on his knuckle, the tattoo on his arm—these are, for identification purposes, "basic" details—but who could really confuse them with the meaningful reality of the one who bears them? Five-petaled corollas and birthplaces do not put us much farther ahead; but, alas, though we know better in our ordinary thought, once we go into an earnestly no-nonsense state of mind, we tend to accept that sort of thing as if it were the heart of the matter.

That is to say: the trite distinction between "objectivity" and "subjectivity" is a fairly accurate image of standard modern habits of thought. The "objective" is the contemporary version of the really real—that which can be measured, weighed, dated, counted, documented, catalogued, and above all *proved,* even to the most skeptical critic. The "subjective" is the rest—treated as only the sort-of-real, the matters of opinion which have only provisional status and must be surrendered as soon as you start getting really serious and hard-headed ("realistic") about it: this includes questions of value, morality, beauty, and virtually everything else that makes things worth more interest than arbitrary curiosity can give them. It goes without saying that the "subjective" is where we really live. We live there gratified and stabilized by the realization that the meaningful objects of our interests or admiration or love have a greater solidity and a firmer bedrock base than the wistful dreams of our longing— but we live there, not in the mere facts. It is not the objective five-petaled corolla but the subjective beautiful rose that we choose as an offering to express our esteem, and the Rilke at whose tomb we may respectfully place it is not essentially the sometime infant of Prague.

In short: to the extent that we let our critical intelligence be intimidated into the standard bias that reduces reality finally to the cash-value of demonstrably objective fact, we are taking wooden nickels. Small wonder that minds thus trained may feel anxious about the Christian reality, which lives where we live and whose objectifiable and provable features naturally turn out to be about as trivial and unrepresentative as the biographical data of the person you most love or the Bureau of Statistics' version of the place you know as home. What is most important in Christian claims eludes the techniques of science and history enough that it can never be adequately established by them. But that simply does not matter: and to allow oneself to be bullied by the temper of the times into thinking that it does matter is to be, in a word, unrealistic.

Look into your own history. Remember what have been the most important moments of your life—those unexpected cross-roads at which things took a decisive turn, those spiritual land-marks from which you still get your bearings about who and where you are. And then think about what these moments would amount to in the objectifying judgment of a detached observer. Some of them may have had an external momentousness about them; but many of them were simply moments that looked like most other moments: as ordinary as weather. What distinguished them was not their factual occasion or their component parts (though these may have been indispensable catalysts for their

71

having been able to take place at all) but the surprising luminousness they took on in the midst of going their own ordinary way. The commonplace observation that suddenly released the great insight; the casual gesture through which you found an unprecedented love; the trivial remark that brought the realization that you had been horribly wrong—how could you possibly demonstrate that these deserved to be considered as valuable as you have found them? How many of them could you prove even happened at all? You shrug it off. That does not matter. You know what went on, and that's sufficient. You know that the sort of reality you *became* through these elusive wisps of history is what really matters, and that cannot be stolen from you by the most skeptical critique—unless you entirely lose the courage to value your life from the inside. And thus there lies within your self-knowing a hidden creed which you have probably never bothered to articulate: in this time and that place, there really happened something in which was revealed a truth too vivid for me to doubt, too important for me to discount, too rich for me to be able to formulate adequately— which I cherish in my memory so that I may not forget myself.

If the claims of Christianity have any substance, this is the way it had to happen there too. That is one of the things that incarnation means: the revelation of God takes place through the ways of man. No magic hand-writing on the wall, no dazzling signs in the sky, no fire from heaven: just the stuff of human lives, ordinary enough that detached bystanders can miss entirely the realization that bursts into bloom within those who are graced to grasp it. Only this time it is not a question merely of the shaping of a private life: these were, like the discoveries of wisdom, the hidden realities to which everyone everywhere was called to come home. Those who found them and lived in them cherished their founding occasions and the staggering truths glimpsed through them, and handed them down carefully to those who followed, as man's memory of the great invitation to more abundant life. This is where and how it all started, the Church's credal memory reminds us: and now that it has happened, we no longer need to go back to where men had been before—from now on, this is where we shall begin. And so, over the centuries of Christian experience, it has continued to happen. The testimony of the Faithed has reaffirmed the living truth of that memory century after century, and the Christian experience in general has proved in the only way possible—by living it out—the enduring validity of that memory as foundation of the Way, the Truth, and the Life.

Let the Faithed therefore rejoice! But the Ungifted? Well, they may rejoice too, but their problem is not solved. If the unshaken confidence of the true believer is vindicated by a more realistic look at all this, the gap that separates the Ungifted from the Church's belief is only reduced, not closed. If the objectification of Christian truth may take place authentically in the creed established and preserved by the belief of the Faithed, that nevertheless leaves the Ungifted precisely where their problem is most acute. To be able to acknowledge the enduring credibility of Christianity's audacious claims is a start, but it is not to be confused with faith. We are back where we started, or nearly so. It is still not clear whether there is any way for the Ungifted to come to terms with a creed which, although they may consider it believable, they do not in fact quite believe.

I spoke earlier of some of the unsatisfactory attempted solutions to this problem—unsatisfactory because they try to make of the creed something different from what it has meant traditionally to Christian believers. These forms of demythologizing fail primarily because of one radical flaw: they attempt to conform the heritage of Christian truth to the beliefs of the Ungifted. But the Ungifted, when understood in accordance with Christian tradition, are exactly the ones who have not enjoyed the privilege of participating fully in that truth; to make them the measure is to settle for a lowest common denominator that falsifies what it seeks to preserve. Still, the instincts of the demythologizing movement are generous and right. The demythologizers have perceived and worked from an important and irreversible realization—that the Ungifted too are true members of the people of God and that the changes in awareness that have revealed them are advances in understanding that cannot be cancelled out. We must find a way of coming to terms with them: there is no returning to the earlier intellectual innocence of the Church.

Some type of demythologizing must necessarily take place. What is wrong with the usual attempts is not the demythologizing itself, but the fact that they mislocate the crucial myth. They strike at the *content* of the Christian creed when what is really called for is rather a demythologizing of the *form* of its profession—that is, the issue is not *what* truths are held, but rather *how* they are held.

The element of traditional understanding that now emerges as an untenable myth, no longer corresponding to what we now perceive as real possibility and therefore needing correction, is not the divinity of Jesus or the physical resurrection or the triunity of God—it is the supposition that all Christians can and should believe in the way that the Faithed believe, that the gift of faith is universally given to individual Christians. The element of truth within this traditional myth is that the Faithed believer shows the fullest type of Christian faith, the paradigmatic case that defines the content of Christian truth. But he is the true type not in the sense of being the normal but rather of being the *normative* type. He is the one whose example keeps us in touch with the fullest kind of confidence and the solidest anchoring of hope in stabilizing fact—just as the saint who is spiritually transfigured in the love of God and of man is the normative and true type of Christian love, inspiring and showing the way to the incomplete rest of us. The Faithed represent the ideal limit: this is the condition of confident belief to which the Christian is invited to aspire. Its relationship to Christian identity is not that it defines what a true Christian claims to *be* but rather what he may *become*. The proper way to demythologize Christian understanding is to recognize that the hope of becoming a true believer is as authentic and characteristic a Christian disposition as the fullness of faith, whatever its imperfections may be.

The problem of sin taught the Christian Church at an early stage of its development the important difference between what the Christian claims to be and what he may hope to become. There was a time in early days, as one can perceive in the Epistle to the Hebrews and in the *Shepherd* of Hermas, when it was supposed that an authentic Christian must be without sin, and that if one sinned after baptism he was lost forever. A difficult growing pain that must have been for many of the weaker brethren; and a great temptation to hide from condemning self-knowledge. But the Church eventually realized that sinners were not so rare, even within the Church, and that they could indeed be forgiven again—and again. But the importance of a similar distinction in the order of faith was not so readily noticed. As I remarked before, it was easier in earlier times to adopt a confident and unquestioning affirmation of the Christian creed; it was easier, within a culture that firmly supported Christian belief, to sustain such an affirmation unwaveringly; and both ecclesiastical discipline and the deeply ingrained attitudes of the community made it difficult for the hidden Ungifted to admit—or even realize—their ungiftedness. A loyalty that is strong, unchallenged, and vigorously encouraged by one's community may easily be mistaken for real faith: so it was in the case of the ordinary Christian in earlier times, the hidden Ungifted. It is not hard to see how the myth of universal Christian faith originated and grew, or why it managed to endure so remarkably long.

But this is a myth with which we can no longer live. In the world of today's Christianity, the previously obscured distinction is forced upon us. The Ungifted are there. They do not believe. We are finally in a position to see that the imperfection of their loyal undisbelief no more disqualifies them than the incompleteness of their love. To join oneself in this way to the belief of the Christian Church is, and always has been, to participate authentically in the life of Christianity.

It is even to participate authentically in Christian faith, although in a form and manner different from that of the individual Faithed believer. For faith is not exclusively a matter of individual dispositions—perhaps not even primarily. As St. Paul forcefully reminds us, the gifts of the Holy Spirit are bestowed upon the Church itself as the corporate body of the faithful. They manifest themselves in individuals, because that is the only way in which they can become effectively present—but they are essentially public and corporate charisms, not private and individual. The gift of prophecy comes to the prophet not for his sake but for the sake of the Church which shares in the gift and its fruits through his prophetic utterance. The gift of teaching is given not for the sake of the teacher but to lead those he teaches out of ignorance into understanding: it is given not to him but to the Church through him. The gift of healing is for the weaknesses of the Church, not for the healer through whom it is given. How far does this corporate principle extend? I suggest that it goes all the way: that the gift by which Christians are able to respond to the love of God is given primarily so that they may bless one another through that love and grow together in grace—and that the belief of the Faithed is given so that through their help the Church itself may be faithful and may remain firm in the truth of God as revealed in Jesus Christ.

Belief, that is to say, is not given fully to each member of the Church. It is a charism bestowed upon the Church itself as the corporate body of the faithful. It must be given to the Church through individuals, but is not given primarily to or for them. When the Church utters its creed, it is expressing the communal experience of faith, enacting the belief of the corporate body as such. The Church's creed is larger in its symbolic significance than any believer's faith: it is the objectification of the living-out of the faith through all of Christian history. It seems to me much more appropriate to think of the "I" of the creed as being the Church itself, the corporate body, than any of the single individuals who may recite it. For although individuals may also believe what the creed formulates for corporate understanding, the liturgical recitation of the creed is something that far transcends the capacities of any individual: it is the Church's official act of grateful remembering, by which it summons up once again the principles of its understanding that have defined its self-consciousness for nearly twenty centuries. No individual can formulate his belief in a manner that speaks for the whole history of Christian experience. Only the Church itself, the faithful body of Christ, can do that. The creed is therefore first and foremost the confession of the Church; if individuals can confess in the same way, that is a happy bonus—for although they may be the indispensable occasion of the Church's being able to sustain its own confession, they are not in themselves, for all their bedrock indispensability, the place in which belief finds its most important home.

In this respect, the creed, as the law of belief for the Church and its people, resembles the ways in which the laws of other peoples have their basis within those other bodies. Those who know the law, the judges and lawyers, serve as the ways in which the whole people stay in tune with the law, serve as the law-consciousness of the corporate body. The rights that are given in the law are given to all who belong to the people, so long as the law is known and remembered by those who are able to master it. It does not matter who they are: as long as they are there, the people possess the gifts of the law. If the gifts of the law have accumulated slowly over a thousand years, they may all be heirs of that thousand years of gathered rights and members of a thousand-year-old-people—without becoming experts in law or history, or even growing old and wise. So it is that the Faithed are the organs of the Church's continuing belief, and those who are members of the Church belong to the belief of the Church and share in it, even though they may not possess its individualized equivalent in private belief.

For the Ungifted to participate in the belief of the Church, without themselves being listed among the agents by whom that belief is sustained, is no more paradoxical than for non-lawyers to participate in the benefits of the law and in the society's fidelity to the law that confers them—or for a loyal member of that society to abide by the policies it has legitimately formed for itself and defend its right to self-determination while still having some honest misgivings about the wisdom or even the justice of some of the ways it has taken. This is neither self-deception nor hypocrisy. It is a recognition of the real difference between private persons and corporate bodies, and of the ways in which they relate to one another. The Ungifted do not cease to be ungifted in belonging to the belief of the Church; they need not pretend either to themselves or to others that they believe what they do not believe. They need only, in joining themselves to the body of the Church and being accepted by it, acknowledge that the normative Christian belief is not their own belief but that of the Church itself. In being so joined to the Church, they are fully entitled to participate in the liturgical recitation of the creed (which is the corporate act of the Church's proclaiming its official belief) without having what they say as members of the Church confused with their private insight and certitude—just as they may solemnly express their solidarity with a political party by contributing, campaigning, and voting in support of it, without this supportive endorsement necessarily implying that they either agree with or even understand fully all the methods and objectives of the group.

It is unlikely that anyone would be inclined to participate in the Church at all without having made at least one rudimentary act of faith—believing that this is a place of life, a body in which one may fruitfully seek the truth to which he is called. This, in the old days, was the way in which a catechumen began his journey into the heart of the Church; and if, in the early stages of his instructions, he still did not or could not believe confidently all that the Church proposed to him as the content of its formal faith, he was nevertheless able to entertain it with reverent seriousness, to trust those who taught it to him, and to hope that through participation in Christian life, he would receive the grace to believe whatever God had called him to believe. Now, what usually happened next is that the catechumen either arrived at a state of conviction about all of it (which was easier to do in earlier times), or thought he had done so (which was also easier), and was received as one to whom the gift of faith had in fact been graciously given. Circumstances long conspired to make this seem to be the way it regularly happened—but under more rigorous scrutiny, it appears that it is now more normal, and probably always has been, for the process to be arrested at the condition of the catechumen, at that level of reverent seriousness and hope and trust in the Faithed through which one who does not yet believe engages in the Church's life of Faith. There stand the Ungifted; they

79

can do no other. Theirs is the condition of the ordinary Christian, even if it may not be that of the perfected Christian. And as long as one recognizes the distinction between the faith of the Church and the faith of its members, it should be clear that there is a place—not a sort of place, or "as it were," but a real and authentic place—within the Church for the Ungifted. Even within the *believing* Church—for as long as we are able to acknowledge reverently that the true faith of the Church is made manifest in its credal heritage, we participate formally in it; and as long as we trust in the integrity of the Faithed, we can participate through them in the truths which it is given to them to know with confidence. In the meantime, living in the reverent hope that we may eventually come to discern and believe whatever is the truth for ourselves, we as private Christian persons may wait patiently in the accepting affirmation of our loyal undisbelief for as long as it shall please God.

VI

"*This Assyrian tribute thing really has me worried,*" *said Ahab.* "*What do you think I should do?*"

"*Thou shalt love the Lord thy God with thy whole heart and thy whole mind and thy whole strength,*" *said Elijah firmly.*

"*That's all very well, Elijah,*" *said Ahab impatiently.* "*And I try in my own small way, believe me. But we have an ultimatum. There are twenty thousand fedayin at the border, waiting to cross over on signal if the tribute isn't paid. You're a man of God: slip me a little advice, for God's sake.*"

"*And thou shalt love thy neighbor as thyself,*" *said Elijah.*

"*Oh, come off it, Elijah,*" *said Ahab exasperatedly.* "*You would have made one hell of a Secretary of State, you really would. I'm sorry now that Jezebel gave me such a hard sell on her brother-in-law. He's only off inspecting our equipment and checking into the possibilities of stalling off this affair long enough to raise the money. But you seem to have these keen suggestions about becoming fast friends with the occupation troops. I just don't know what I'd do without you.*"

"*There's no need to get sarcastic,*" *said Elijah.* "*I'm trying to help, in my own way.*"

"*I appreciate that, Elijah,*" *said Ahab,* "*I really do. But I wish just once you'd come up with something practical.*"

"*I guess,*" *said Elijah,* "*it all depends on what you want to practice.*"

On Being in the World, but out of It

THE loyal undisbelief with which the Ungifted participate in the faith of the Church is enough to make them part of faithful Christianity; but that's not all there is to the current form of the perennial problem of the Ungifted. Even after they rediscover the enduring credibility of Christianity and find a way of belonging to it which does not compromise either their own integrity or that of traditional Christian self-understanding, there remain some important misgivings. Most of them come from one basic perception that itches and festers within them in a hundred different ways: it is that the Christianity they know simply does not seem to have a great deal to do with the world in which they live.

How well has Christianity succeeded in showing to the modern world a face that seems to belong there? Consider: the tradition I grew up in preferred to build its churches in imitation of styles of architecture that flourished some six centuries ago, clothed its leading religious personnel in garments made in styles fashionable as recently as six centuries ago (that is, for more casual everyday wear: when it was a question of more solemn occasions, like saying Mass, such new-fangledness was rejected for the more sober modes of some thousand years earlier), and did as much of its praying as as it could afford to in a language which has not been spoken as anyone's native tongue for maybe fifty generations. Of course, it was not exclusively confined to manners quite so archaic. In some of its less formal services, it shared with other Christian churches the daring tendency to creep within a century of our own time. But even then, the effect of mid-nineteenth-century hymns and artwork was kept from giving an impression of frivolous novelty by the steadying use of a brand of English that has been, in some of its features, three hundred years out of normal uses, with a rich enough seasoning of "thou hast" and "vouchsafe" and "hallowed" to keep even the standard grace before meals safely out of the reach of children—and of many puzzled adults as well.

I loved it that way. It made everything as exotic and mysterious as incense, and out of it came a sense of the divine presence —or if not quite that, at least a sense of the grandeur that would belong to it when and if it would come to rest among us. But there was a price of irrelevance built in. If, in order to function religiously, one is obliged to take on for religious occasions an attitude, a set of gestures and postures, even a grammar that has no function outside this context, one is taking on an unbridged and perhaps unbridgeable relevance gap—a gap of not one but several generations—over which the different modes of one's experience have serious difficulty communicating. If your native country is the everyday world, an exotic world of religion then becomes a foreign land which may be refreshing to visit but in which you do not really care to settle down. Among the quiet and homely grace of the resolvedly anti-modern Amish people, with their nineteenth-century clothing and machinery and manners, you may be able to suppose that it would be better to stay there than to return to your usual life. But you know very well that you can't have both. It is not a question of interpreting the one by the other. The discontinuity is virtually total: it is either/or. And so it was in many traditional forms of Christianity. One could be of the world, and stay just enough in touch with Christianity to keep from getting totally lost; or, if one desired to live a fully Christian life, it was assumed that this meant leaving this world and transferring one's citizenship to the other one in a vocation that renounced the ordinary world as if it were irredeemably incompatible with authentic Christianity.

Mind you, I'm not saying that this was the official and universal position taken explicitly by spokesmen for Christianity. It surely was proclaimed by some; but even if they were not in the majority, this was nevertheless the picture that we used to absorb as our over-all impression of how things really worked. Even those who were fortunate enough to discover that living Christianity was not measured exclusively by devoted otherworldliness were still stuck with a problem of relevance built into the discontinuity between their world and that in which their religion defined itself. Unless they had undergone an arduous process of transformation in the basic ways their minds worked, their self-understanding was still based on the ways of the world, and was to that extent still unblessed and unacknowledged by the ways of Christianity. Their notions of what real joy and real sorrow and real confidence were like were not derived from the sorts of experience which the Church said were the true ones; as persons, they came to know about themselves in terms of their central nervous systems and emotional balance, and strove for a sense of independent and unique identity—while as Christians, they were compounds of body and soul, encouraged to transcend mere individuality in order to become like Christ. For many, this was a bewildering double standard: the great moment of jubilant accomplishment might be, from a divine viewpoint, sinful pride; the most agonized and destructive self-hatred could be thought of as a spiritual blessing of humility; and the way in which one consciously experienced and evaluated one's life was understood to be so discontinuous with the invisible order of grace as to be simply an unreliable guide.

It is not only hard to live in two such alien worlds. For most people, it is impossible, even if one is careful to arrange things so as to make them separate but equal, in the hope of eliminating the conflict between them. That never works. As long as they have not really come to terms with one another, one of them must finally have a last word in determining where we really live. And the odds are in favor of this world, because it is our basic place, the land of our mother tongue. It is meet and just that we should retain a special language, hallowed by a tradition of liturgical solemnity, for communal prayer on highly formal religious occasions: meet and just, right, and availing unto salvation. But if we do this only, we are lost from ourselves. If we do not pray also, less formally and officially, in the very language we use for our pain and our joy among our families and friends, then our love of God cannot quite come home to us. It can only knock at the outer gate, waiting for the door to be opened that will admit it to our native land. The same is true with our thinking. There is an important place for technical theology, as there is for scientific meteorology. But we must also be able to chat about the weather of our spiritual understanding, in a way that makes the truth belong all the way down to the roots of our life's meaning. Something dazzling happens when one encounters a successful translation of traditional mystery into its closest homely counterpart—as if the old familiar material has suddenly and for the first time finally settled onto the bedrock, the really real.

Christianity has, however, been oddly reluctant to get itself that well translated. Even in the literal sense of the word, for there has been a curious tendency in English versions of the Bible, even within the current generation (though diminishingly), to cling to archaic language that keeps the message from mingling on really familiar terms with the way we actually speak and think. Of course every generation tries translating a few gospel parables into its own current slang; but specializing in the language which we tend to reserve for our most casual thoughts does not revivify, it only trivializes. Similar attempts at instant relevance go on around us now, attempting to close a gap in religious understanding and purpose with a wave of a hand, or of a peace sign. I see slogans painted on walls: God is Groovy, Jesus is Right On, Christianity is Where It's At. Out of sight. Or is it out of mind? Often both, I suspect: for while a little of such rhetorical maneuvering may be eye-catchingly effective, in the long run the attempt to promote an image of a Swinging Lord is no less bogus than the commercials from which the trick was learned. If pursued consistently, it betrays and trivializes what it deals with. And if it is, as often turns out to be the case, just a door-opener for a basically unmodified Old Style Christianity, then it is nothing but new patches on old garments—and we have it on the best authority what *that* sort of thing leads to.

No, the gap cannot be closed at the level of simple translations, whether they be of catchwords or of Bibles. For one thing, the translation does not make the original obsolete: it merely helps to reduce its distance from our life. And for another thing, the dissociation has taken place on too large a scale to be so easily answered. The whole range of manners, modes of thought, values, aspirations—virtually all of life has been allowed to develop in two quite discontinuous paths of understanding, with far too little history of conversation between them to have established an adequate common ground. There has been too little mutuality for Christianity to be properly equipped to speak directly to the bedrock self-understanding of modern lives, or for modern secular consciousness to see itself as pointing toward Christianity. Those whose lives have been carefully put together in the midst of this estrangement must find it nearly impossible to avoid the suspicion—even, at times, the conviction—that Christianity has too little to do with where they live.

It isn't that they live in the wrong place or the wrong time, or even in the wrong way. On the contrary, they have declined the option of beating a Spiritual Retreat from the religiously unsettling features of our time, and live in the only world that has any chance of being thoroughly real for them, and usually in some form of earnest engagement with its present agonies and urgencies. And although the consciously ungifted Christians cover pretty well the whole spectrum of humanity, they are on the whole neither ignorant nor inexperienced: they include a goodly proportion of the more alert and generous, who have a fairly well-developed sense of the present needs of contemporary men—against which the nature of traditional Christianity does not seem to measure up in a very distinguished way, either in past performance or in promise for the future. In a hundred ways, the active Ungifted are haunted by the problem of Christian irrelevance.

In one form, the felt irrelevance of Christianity has been acute for quite a while. Only it didn't use to be urgent. The more respectable and less energetic Christian churches have been subjected to massive doses of spiritual boredom over the last century, an experience which inspired and assisted them to develop a style of Christianity that was dutiful, decorous, and—aside from its capacity to gobble up people's Sunday mornings—almost totally ineffectual. Of course, in times when the outlook of even fairly generous-spirited persons tended to be more restricted and localized—when the dimensions of the world seemed more awesome and distant, and its good Samaritans did not necessarily feel responsible for all of its sufferings and injustices—it did not seem quite so scandalous for churches to lounge around like the spayed and toothless housepets of a cozy and congenial establishment. The tension of Christian irrelevance was not so keenly felt before, but its existence was one of the facts of life—and even one of the more satisfying facts of life to those who liked to keep their Christianity tame. No need for it to raise its ugly head too high into questions of social justice. You may remember that when Pope Leo XIII advanced in *Rerum Novarum* what now seem like rather elementary and modest notions of the responsibilities of employers toward employees, the general reaction was to suggest that business is business, and His Holiness would do better to mind his own and go say his rosary.

The felt irrelevance is not new. But the widespread additional feeling of indignation that finds such irrelevance an outrageous scandal is more of a novelty. It is also a sign of life. And those who feel it most keenly are quite aware of that fact—which makes the crisis sharper even while it makes the situation more hopeful. If earlier attempts of Christianity to muscle into relevance were regarded in some quarters as something of an impertinence, those who found it so were nevertheless able to be tolerant and forgiving. The respectful esteem in which Sunday-morning Christendom held the weekly visits of their venerable though eccentric religion was sufficient to make it willing to overlook the indiscretion of Christianity's occasionally trying to make a great difference. But those who now resent the inertia which the churches developed in those days are less ready to be reconciled with a Christianity that doesn't know its place. As they look at the poor and the sorrowful and those who hunger and thirst after justice, they know that when the Truth really comes, it will make them free. Any movement or government or religion that does not long for, and work for, that liberation has missed out on an important part of the Truth. And then they look to the history of the Christian churches, and begin to wonder if the Gospel has yet found a home. By their fruits you shall know them. What do we know of Christianity when we evaluate what it has brought about among its people? Set aside the changes that have been wrested from nominally Christian societies by purely secular revolutions and power-blocs, and what do you have as the specifically Christian achievement in bringing among men a true reflection of the mercy and the justice of God? You have something uncomfortably close to the situation of Peter just before cock-crow.

Not everyone is willing to wait until the actual crowing of the cock brings the bitter tears of repentance and the bedrock-solid reformed purposefulness. The Christian Ungifted may have Christianity in their bones, but they respond with ready instinctiveness to signs of authenticity elsewhere too, and find an impressive spiritual attraction in some of the other movements which seem more vitally responsive to the needs of our time than does Christianity. They are being constantly offered supplementary alternatives—and it sometimes appears that they are being wooed by rivals.

Rivals: not just alternatives or imitators. For in the last couple of centuries, the West has undergone another important new experience. For the first time, there were major movements of reform and salvation that appealed to human generosity directly and did not operate under the protective umbrella of Christianity. Earlier social holy wars were fought out between Christian groups—but more recently it has been the French republican freethinkers versus the clerical establishment, the Marxist communists against the Church-linked Tsarist government, the Maoists and the Black Muslims against a society frequently characterized as WASP—that is, in terms of white racism and its supporting Christian religion. Not only has Christianity failed to distinguish itself in the leadership of movements that strive for the liberation of the oppressed—it winds up, with painful frequency, being characteristically associated with the opposition. On the basis of the record, it is understandable if some of those who long for the deliverance of man from man come to the conclusion that Christianity is better honored in the breach than in the observance, that the Gospel does better outside the Church than within it, and best in circles that are not only non-Christian but decidedly anti-Christian. It sometimes looks as if history is gathering together another vast ironic Either/Or: choose Christianity and betray the Gospel, or choose the Gospel and reject the unfaithful Church.

The crisis of Christian relevance, intensified by considerations like these, is perhaps even more acute than the crisis of belief. The Church promises, and even lays claim to, a more abundant life. But such a claim, when tested for vitality against the quickened pulse of contemporary ideals, does not seem to ring true. In the face of the needs and urgencies that burst constantly forth from the new things that we find ourselves and our world becoming, the Christian heritage looks increasingly like a school of clumsy incapacity. The Churches' tendency toward solving the problem by Spiritual Retreat or New Patches is an intolerable avoidance of it rather than a solution, a retreat not only from the issue but from the very forms of contemporary vitality through which it might be met. Whatever dreaming Christianity may have done about radical justice or human brotherhood, it is no longer to its credit. The dream becomes a betrayal when it is time to wake up. It is no longer obvious that Christianity deserves anything better than the nostalgic minor concessions of As It Were—or even the bolder rejection of the Post-Christian Leap.

And thus many of the Ungifted go about what they take to be their Father's business, working through the organizations and movements that seem best equipped and best disposed to be effective in it—Oxfam, the Black Panthers, the Peace Committees. These are built to order, to meet new needs; among them, the Church can take on something of the same picturesque but nonfunctional archaism of the Old Firehouse or the County Creamery which the city fathers may or may not allow to be torn down to make way for a new office complex, depending on how practicality and nostalgic sentiment work out their competing demands.

If the trial of Christian relevance is conducted according to the most clear-headed judgment of the most uncompromisingly practical humanity of our time, there can hardly be any question of the verdict. The churches will be declared bankrupt, and it will only remain to be decided whether the proper sentence should be death, exile, or confinement in irremediable poverty to a perpetual debtors prison for the rest of its—probably mercifully short—life.

But if the trial of relevance is conducted brusquely and exclusively according to the canons of modern humanism, as is often the case in the informal trials through which Christianity is judged irrelevant, then it is a kangaroo court. The demand which it embodies is unreal and desperate, like the discussions that went on some years ago attempting to discover what it meant to be a Christian physicist. If Christianity is condemned for being inhabited by unfashionable kinds of sinners, the sluggish and conservative, and for lacking the righteousness to which its activist judges can lay claim, there is an ancient name for that sort of judgment: it is Pharisaism.

There is no denying or dodging the charges it lays upon the Publican Church. Christianity has been too preoccupied about being the Truth and has been negligent about developing and preserving its self-understanding as Way and Life. The churches have a great deal to learn—and a great deal to remember. As always. The Church has always been incomplete, has always been insufficient, has always (whether admitting to it or not) been publican: these are among the permanent facts of Christian life and history. They are not in themselves proof of either obsolescence or senility. They are evidence of limitations on what may legitimately be asked and what may reasonably be expected.

91

It seems to me right and just, similarly, to prod the world's universities into greater direct involvement in pressing contemporary problems—but it does nobody any good to pretend that it is within their competence to eliminate suffering. And the faults that remain must be charged where they belong: for while it is true in a way that Christianity has failed, it is probably more accurate to say that it hasn't really been seriously attempted yet.

If things had followed their proper course, the world's leadership in the implementation of the social dimensions of the Gospel would have fallen always to the Christian churches. There would have been no need for revolutionary rivals to come to the rescue of oppressed humanity. Alas, that is not how it has worked out. If Christianity were a political party, or a social philosophy, or a club for economic reform, the disappointing performance of the churches would probably be firm enough ground for repudiating it altogether as a way that does not work. It is often treated as if this were the case. Jesus is characterized as essentially a social reformer bringing liberation to the poor of Israel; the emphasis is laid on the Johannine observation that if you do not love your brother whom you see, you cannot love the invisible God; the president of one of the most powerful and representative Catholic laymen's organizations in the United States draws an enormous ovation from the membership when he announces that we want a Church that will end poverty and racial discrimination and put a stop to war—and a day or so later, one of the major commissions of the organization drafts a policy paper that begins by stating that "The fundamental mission of the Church is to promote the personal and social fulfillment of man."

If the twentieth-century mind is set especially in terms of science and history, twentieth-century moral conscience and sense of value are ordered particularly toward the personal and social fulfillment of man. I'm not complaining. I enjoy the advantages of a time when it is presumed that anyone who is really aware and adequately sensitive will be concerned about social justice and the pursuit of personal vitality. I like it here. But I don't think it's so good to be entirely swallowed by modern styles. On the intellectual side, this results (as I suggested earlier) in a relatively thin and impoverished view of reality, however sturdy. On the side of values, there is a strong tendency in a similar direction.

What is it we really want when we take our stand for the personal and social fulfillment of man? In generous but fuzzy ways, we want everything good, everything happy. But when it really comes to the pinch of practicality and specific action, the expansive generosity of our subjective horizons narrows down to a clearer objectified focus: we want to see that every man has his share of the pie and enough elbow-room to make use of it, free of all the political, social, and economic oppressions under which he now suffers; and we want each of us to be able to be himself, to do his own thing, to take his place among the *honest* people who are, whatever anyone may say, really where it's at:

> *I guess people would say that I am too attached to them,*
> *Or that I should love them "in Christ"*
> *And of course, I don't love them "in Christ"*
> *I love them as they are.*
> *Don't touch a thing about them, leave them alone.*
> *I don't know what this "in Christ" bit really means.*

This is a noble longing—perhaps even a holy one—so far as it goes. But it doesn't go very far in terms of the real possibilities of human value, at least in the ways I usually find it to be understood. If you will permit me a moment of ugly candor, I will confess that this sort of aspiration often seems to me to be a betrayal. It does not ordinarily seem to go farther than to try to win for the poor and oppressed the same chance to be corrupted by relative ease and opulence that we lament in the middle class, or to win for each individual the chance to parade his inadequacies and be proud of them. I believe deeply that poverty and oppression are dehumanizing, and that freedom to be oneself is important. But I also believe that there is no virtue so overrated, and perhaps none so cheap, as sincerity; and that to be rescued from squalor is only a beginning, not a completion. What our time's spontaneous generosity asks for men and from men is enormously important as a start toward peace and justice—but it tends to be only the simplest minimum, and is as a total vision ultimately worthy of neither the rescuers nor those whom they would save. And when, as is often the case, the pursuit of the personal and social fulfillment of man is more tolerant of a terrorism that hastens the process than of an inertia that retards it, the unworthiness has reached dangerous proportions.

Poor impoverished creatures that we are, our shrunken imaginations have shrivelled our sense of relevance to their own size. But the question of relevance cuts two ways. One way is obvious, and is voiced shrilly everywhere these days: what's in it for *me?* What can this deliver to my preferences and preoccupations? What's the cash value on my market? This frankly lays it on the line—but that line then becomes a boundary beyond which one is much less likely to grow, having already staked out for himself the territory which defines him. Unless this kind of question is complemented with the other side of the coin, it becomes an invitation to stunted growth.

There is, however, another side to the question of relevance. It is that which looks to the values and hopes and ambitions which have been sifted and cherished by centuries of discriminating human experience and asks a question which we have nearly forgotten how to ask: how relevant to all this have I managed to become? How does my image look in this mirror of accumulated humanity? What judgment falls upon me here?

For if we pause long enough to stop begging the question about the matter, and arrive at the point where we can really ask who it is that is on trial, we may hear it whispered gently in our ears that it is not Christianity but ourselves. "I don't know what this 'in Christ' bit really means," saith the preacher. Fine, so far. Typical dilemma of the Ungifted and the uninstructed. So what do we conclude? If one is honed exclusively to the modern cutting-edge, the probable conclusion is the one that seems to take place in this little verse-prayer: "in Christ" is a "bit" which "of course" I don't buy—I love people as they are, in a real way, not like that. But if one has at least partially avoided being imprisoned in the clamorous arrogance of modern illusory self-sufficiency, it just may occur that this is a confession rather than a condemnation, and that a way of speaking about love that has been revered and developed over centuries of carefully reflective Christian experience is perhaps not altogether proved to be nonsense by the mere fact of my not knowing what it really means. My incomprehension may even suggest that I have something to learn. Do I then ignore it, on the ground that it and I are not yet of the same style? Or do I find a way of reducing it to what I already am? Or do I, possibly, try to grow to meet it—try to acquire a relevance that I now appear to lack?

"Well, if you *need* that sort of thing . . ." says the unrepentant and unyielding spirit of modernity. O sly sabotage! This is the last-ditch stand by which tough contemporariness evades the responsibility of thinking seriously about religious questions. Just pretend that the whole thing can be reduced to questions of need—implicitly, questions of maturity—and declare yourself among the grown-up and independent. No need, no relevance. Religion is for the unweaned.

There is an element of truth in that position—rather in the way that one may say that some people "need" challenging responsibilities. For some, it is true, power and excitement are obsessions; some people are psychologically unable to live out their lives in quiet and modest jobs without going berserk—while others, more composed, can be content with whatever turns out to be convenient. Bravo composure, and pity the poor compulsive. But that's not the whole story. There are others who seek out challenging responsibilities not because they "need" to do so, but because they see in this a way of getting more out of their lives—and more *into* their lives as well. It is no fairer to suppose that they are feeding compulsions than to suppose that the more detached and unambitious people are merely lazy. Similarly, some people need religion; but what has that got to do with judging the value of religion? Does it reduce it to being nothing more than the need it sometimes is called upon to answer? Or imply that only need can take one there? Not if you keep your head clear. Need defines only a special type of relevance, not the whole thing.

If we are to face the crisis of Christian relevance fairly, we must face up to the most radical form of the question—one far more radical than the contemporary feeling of the needlessness or payoff-impracticality of Christianity. It is this: how relevant are my life and my understanding of its possibilities to the accumulated wisdom of nearly two thousand years of Christian experience?

Wisdom: hardly a groovy word these days, but not a bad test of one's freedom from the oppression of spiritual fashions. Wisdom may not succeed in rescuing the poor, or finding a way to put an end to war; it may not win elections or win friends and influence people or do its own thing with flair—but it makes all the difference in the quality of life. Christianity is not a recipe for "the personal and social fulfillment of man," at least not what is ordinarily meant by such words in modern political circles. To treat it as if it were is a hopeless blunder, like trying to make a religion out of the army, or maybe even like trying to make an army out of religion. But Christianity is, in the face it turns toward even the Ungifted, *at least* a wisdom. *That* sort of personal and social blessing it knows something about, and continues to offer. In doing so, it retains its claim to relevance as long as it lives, and it can die only in the way a wisdom dies: by being abandoned.

Christianity was never easy. And it was probably rarely obvious. I suppose that all the Ungifted—and perhaps a goodly share of the Faithed too—have secretly envied St. Paul, driven relentlessly by the demands of the Gospel but at least fully secure in the lightning of conviction that had struck him on the road to Damascus. For all the shipwrecks and scourging and perils, we sometimes suspect that his life was easier to deal with than the way it usually is for the Ungifted—the difficult and tiresome business of opting continually to sustain a Christian identity that has not transfigured us. But, like the unwise who try to absorb something of wisdom, we must start from where we are. Most of us are rather clumsy beginners. We may struggle on and become better—or we may quit. Christianity has not really been imposed on us; we could probably shake it off if we wish to do so. It has already been weakened, after all, by having been deprived of our courageous dedication to what it demands of our active lives. We could allow it to die to us altogether merely by withholding from it the faith, hope and love on which its remaining power and vitality in our lives depend. But let us be clear at least about this: it is our choice that must decide the relevance of Christianity, and the relevance of ourselves.

Whatever may have been imposed upon St. Paul by the revelation that burst upon him, the Christianity of the Ungifted is not imposed. It is there by gracious invitation only. For us to suppose that the authority of Christianity is obliged to make itself felt in us before we decide is to misunderstand who we are.

We are precisely those in whom that does not happen. And to presume that the relevance of Christianity may be fully apparent before we make our choice is to misunderstand both Christianity and the human condition. That is what this choice is all about. The world is not given to us already defined. We have no way of escaping responsibility for the formation of the sort of place in which we live and find our meaning. Even if we settle for the objectified world of modern scientific vision and dictionary thinking, we have chosen by default. The crisis of relevance is the crisis of our decision; that to which we make ourselves relevant will live.

So if we're looking for a way to raise the minimum wage, develop our talents, or alleviate suffering, there are schools and organizations and movements that specialize in such worthy works. Christendom will probably give its encouragement and blessing (at least moderately enlightened Christendom—but admittedly not all of it is yet very enlightened), but is not to be expected to do the work for us. What Christianity offers has something to do with all that and encourages our striving for it, since Christianity has to do with all the ways in which a man may be blessed by his brothers or his Lord; but its ultimate relevance is deeper and less particular. A Way that embraces many paths, a Truth that is beyond techniques, a Life that is more fundamental than all programs: not a technology or a strategy but—at least—a wisdom. We must take it or leave it as such. The choice is open. We don't *need* to accept. We are free to settle for less—much less.

VII

"*All right,*" *said Jezebel,* "*do whatever the hell you like. Kick all the prophets of Baal out of the kingdom, for all I care. I'm fed up with the whole thing.*"

"*No need to get so upset,*" *said Ahab.* "*Sure, I'm a Yahwist, and Elijah expects me to take a firm stand about Baal and Ashteroth. But I'm a king too, and I've got responsibilities to my people. Not everybody is ready to see it Elijah's way. I'm prepared to be tolerant.*"

"*Don't bother for me,*" *said Jezebel.* "*I'm sick and tired of rationalizing my way into orthodoxy. Oh, I can argue as well as anyone that my misgivings don't disqualify me. I can even get romantic about the way Baal and Ashteroth are meaningful representations of the power of the cosmos and the beautiful cycle of fertility and all that. But who needs them? Better to let it all go and concentrate on where you really are.*"

"*That's what I'm trying to do by* not *letting it all go,*" *said Ahab.*

"*Pooh,*" *said Jezebel.* "*You want to cling to your childhood, that's all. Yours and your people's, I should say, since you're just as sentimental about folklore as you are about your Bar Mitzvah. Cut the apron strings, kiddo. Time to put away the things of a child.*"

"*One never really can,*" *said Ahab.* "*I mean, when you grow up you quit lisping and lose interest in dolls and outgrow your silly ideas about where babies come from . . .*"

"*Mine were never as bizarre as the truth,*" *interjected Jezebel.*

"... *but your child-self,*" *continued Ahab,* "*is still in there somewhere, like the inner rings of a tree, still giving shape to the rest of you. You still belong to it even as an adult, no matter how much you may try to fight it.*"

"*Bull,*" *said Jezebel.*

"*Well,*" *mused Ahab,* "*I notice that when you get a little sloshed you almost always wind up talking about the summers you spent in the mountains as a kid. And if someone sings a Sidonian lullaby, you simply go to pieces. Even when you're sober.*"

"*Okay, so I'm sentimental,*" *said Jezebel petulantly.* "*And immature. Is that what you want me to say?*"

"*Not at all,*" *said Ahab.* "*You sell yourself short. And you sell the mountains and the lullabies short too. And, as a matter of fact, I'm not sure which is worse.*"

Gathering the Ungifted

IN the Bad Old Days, when one discovered that he was not really a believer, he supposed that he had died to positive Christianity. All that remained were various ways of being buried: drop out entirely, shunned and lamented by family and friends; pretend that you believe; or shrivel up silently in some dark corner of the Christian world and wait for the end. Ignorance is pain, not bliss; and the tragic pain of the old Ungifted was the anguish of supposing that either God had rejected them or they had rejected God—when the real meaning of their undisbelief was ordinarily only that they were not called to be pillars of the Church's faith. If Ungiftedness is properly understood, there is no need for anyone to undergo that pain ever again.

In the Bad New Days, on the other hand, when one discovers that Christianity is not groovy, he occasionally supposes that it is dead. All that remains then are the various ways of burying it: split the Christian scene entirely; hang on in an attitude of detached patronizing (or hostile) boredom—or try to make Christianity groovy. Ignorance can also be anesthesia. The most effective form is self-ignorance, but there is also something numbing about being unaware of the history of spiritual undertakings and how they can remind who we are about who we may be. If relevance is properly understood, there is no need for anyone to undergo the self-impoverishment of such spiritual provinciality ever again.

That is to say: the problem of belief and the problem of relevance are not what they often seem. In their basic and frequent forms, they appear to raise insuperable impediments to the continuation of Christian life, but it is nothing of the sort. All the same, that is not all there is to it. The absence of impediments is hardly sufficient ground for marriage. Even if what I do *not* believe need not necessarily estrange me from Christianity, and even if what Christianity does *not* accomplish or attempt need not estrange it from me, what *positive* basis is there for my participation?

The answer, if it is to be found at all, must be discovered in the same roots from which the problem sprang in the first place: belief and relevance. These are not everything, but they are indispensable beginnings. Not even the Ungifted are exempt. But neither are they excluded. And when they search out exactingly what they really believe and what really matters to them, they may discover more than they had supposed.

Not that such a survey is an easy job. We have wonderful ingenuity for hiding from ourselves anyway, and when you complicate the situation by adding the traditional uneasiness and guilt experienced by the Ungifted, and the self-stabilizing counterreaction that often accompanies it, the truth may become rather hard to track down. This man, having become insecure about his relationship to Christianity, may decide that what he really believes in is Religion, and that Christianity had been for him little more than a special instance of it; and some time later he wakes up to realize that although he may enjoy studying it, in fact he does not believe in "religion" as such but is bored to death by trying to practice it—and that the only thing his heart really finds interesting about religion is that it is a general aspect of Christianity. Another man, zealous for social justice, may think that the laziness of the churches has divorced his world from theirs and proved that they have nothing valuable to say to him—only to find, when he studies himself more exactingly, that what animates and motivates his conscience is really after all not instinctive sympathy but a specifically Christian vision of human dignity, embedded in the marrow of his mind.

For that feeling in the bones that links the Ungifted to Christianity, deep and sturdy as a remembrance of home, is not mere nostalgia. It is the pulse of their real beliefs and the breath of their true longing: it is an echo of self-knowledge.

This is not to say that the Ungifted are really secretly faithed after all. The faith I am speaking of now is not the heavenly gift, but only that ordinary act of self-definition by which all men establish their engagement with their lives, and through which avengers and revolutionaries are produced as well as Christians. It is real, and it is theirs, but it behaves rather differently from that of the Faithed.

For instance: in the course of the past century's intensive scholarly investigation into the origins of Christianity, it became clear that all was not well between the traditional view of Christian beginnings and the critical study to which it was being subjected. Increasingly, it appeared that the claims that Jesus seems to be making for himself in the Gospels were perhaps not historically accurate remembrances but rather projections of the early Church's belief back into the time before the crucifixion—placing their discoveries about him in an earlier setting, so that they could come under the explicit authority of Jesus' own public ministry. Increasingly, it appeared that the disciples' understanding of Jesus at the time of the crucifixion had really been more like that of Cleopas, who describes Jesus in the last chapter of the Gospel of Luke as "a man, a prophet, powerful in work and in word before God and all the people ... the one we hoped would be the liberator of Israel." Which is an impressive tribute, to be sure—but rather short of the picture given elsewhere in the Gospels, with Jesus' explicit predictions of his redemptive death and glorious resurrection, with the assurances of his authority and the hints of his divinity. In short, it began to look as if perhaps the divine and redemptive Christ who had for so long been the object of the belief of the Christian church had not really been manifest in the pre-crucifixion Jesus after all.

Confronted by a dissociation between the Church's belief and the scholars' view of the pre-crucifixion Jesus—a dissociation that threatened to undermine the very basis of Christianity —the intelligent belief of Faithed scholars responded with a critical distinction between the Jesus of History and the Christ of Faith. What finally matters to Christian faith, they asserted, is the divine redeemer encountered by the early Church in what they took (accurately or inaccurately) to be the risen Jesus. This is the Christ of Faith, whose saving presence the believer may still encounter more than nineteen centuries later—invisible to the unbelieving world at large but real and powerful to the eye of faith. And as for the pre-crucifixion Jesus of History, the claim went on, he does not matter. It does not matter who he is or what he was like or even whether we know anything at all about him: the Christ of Faith is immediately accessible without requiring an appeal to spent history. Transformed and living in the Christ of Faith, the Christian need not worry about the Jesus of History, whose career does not much matter for faith.

Now, this may be all very well for the Faithed. If grace offers them a short-cut into higher levels of understanding, they can perhaps afford to disdain the historical Jesus. But be that as it may, it is at any rate clear that this luxury is not available to those who have not been liberated from the guidance of a spe-cifically human judgment and understanding.

What works in the case of such people? As I have already suggested, earlier on, they are usually endowed with something of an instinctive taste for genuine good news and a ready disposi-tion to respond to it. That seems to me a fairly neutral and standard way of putting it; but standard ways of putting things are often a bit misleading. So it is, I think, with usual remarks about the transmission of good news, whether it be in the form of a philosophy or a wisdom or a gospel. That is, it is usually dealt with as if the message itself is exclusively what matters, and that it is quite indifferent whether it arrives through a teacher or in a plain unmarked envelope. I do not think that this is true to the facts; and although I will spare you my elaborate argument on the matter, I ask you to test its conclusion against your own experience: isn't it the case that your awakenings to good news come characteristically through some *personal* intervention or mediation?

I don't mean that the ideas that turned you on were originated by or transmitted by some individual. Obviously—few of us have ever actually tried the monkeys-on-typewriters technique of securing revelation. What I mean is rather that the priority of your response characteristically goes to the bearer rather than the message—that the sort of "Aha!" experience you have translates not so much "These are important considerations" as "This guy is getting through to me," not "These ideas are sound" but "He really seems to be on to something there." Not the abstract but the incarnate word, the utterance that proceeds from an authoritative presence. The personal authority may be vivid and immediate, as when Jesus stunned his old neighbors by speaking "with authority and not the way the scribes speak," or it may be only oblique and suggested, the way we can still get a faint glimpse of that authoritative presence in the Gospels; but it is, I think, the catalytic agent that makes all the difference.

The Faithed recognize this in another way. For them, the catalyst is the preacher of the Word, to whom grace gives authority to awaken faith in Christ. But the Ungifted are precisely those in whom that does not happen. The authoritative mediation of the preacher of the Word is not, in their case, adequate. They find some supplementary help elsewhere—in the evident authority of exemplary Christian lives, in the trusted (even if not communicated) belief of the vividly Faithed. A valid Christianity can indeed be grounded in these recognitions all by themselves, since they are enough to establish one's beginning belief in the authenticity of Christianity. In fact, the job of figuring out *what* one believes may often be made immeasurably easier— and more accurate—if one begins by taking an inventory of *whom* one believes in, and then determines the rest from there. And if it transpires that your degree of belief in Christianity is simply and exclusively a function of your belief in certain Christians of your immediate or historical acquaintance, this is a legitimate foundation. Even a traditional one. And if the Christ of traditional Christian belief, the Christ of the Faithed, boggles the Ungifted mind, there remains another point of appeal in the bedrock origins of Christianity.

For one of the curious paradoxes of Ungiftedness is that it tends to transpose the terms of the Faithed rather than abandoning them, and recovers a foundation on a more basic level. Even when seen stripped of the elements that belong to the gifted faith of the early (and later) Church, the Jesus of the Gospels can continue to speak good news with authority into the lives of the Ungifted. For them, the Christ of the Church's devotion may only be grasped indirectly, as the Christ of History that gives meaning and coherence to the history of the Church—but at the root of his emergence, the Ungifted may perceive the Jesus of Faith.

Ungifted Cleopas remains right. The Jesus of Faith who was publicly manifest to him through the mere Jonah-sign of his words and deeds remains the mediator of good news and the authentic foundation of Christian belief—accessible even to the Ungifted. This too is offered to us, not imposed, and in this and what may follow from it, it is every man for his own conscience and consciousness. But I fancy that I am fairly typical of the

Ungifted, and on that hunch I venture to acknowledge that it is wonderful to discover the congruence of the Gospel borne by the Jesus of Faith with all that I could ultimately wish to become; and when I look further, I discover as well the revealing importance of the Christian experience as history reports it, and the rightness of what the Christian body in its best and most lucid moments has tried to be and to give to the world. When I survey what I really believe, and look at it in the mirror of Christianity, I find that the same image is given back—as in a glass, darkly, to be sure: but it is an image that I experience as a guiding judgment and a calling home. It is this kind of wisdom with which I long to be wise.

That may seem like a rather fluffy way of putting it. Do not let me mislead you. What I am trying to express is neither a dream nor a nostalgia, though it is an experience ample enough to bless and honor both of these as well. It is not a way to avoid facing up to what I guess to be the truth, but a way to arrive at a greater honesty than I can achieve by sheer confession of insufficiency. If I am to take full and detailed responsibility for who I am and where I am, I cannot overlook the fact that facing up to the Christianity that has always lived with me delivers to me something valuable in myself, something that I have never been able to receive at other hands. I cannot deny that when I listen reverently to the testimony of traditionally Christian modes of consciousness, I find in them a peculiar ability to affirm and encourage what I recognize as life, to value what is true and life-giving within this and other contexts while transcending what is provincial and self-deceiving in this and all individual moments. I find a perspective that is both fruitful and wise. I am not talking about personal or antiquarian nostalgia. I am talking about what lives in the best moments of my ongoing experience *now,* about who and what I understand myself to be when I am most free. And then above all I know that the

Christian people are my nation, the Christian language the mother-tongue in which I do my most adequate thinking. A problem of relevance? If these considerations are not central to the question of relevance, then I cannot think how the term is to be used.

All this may still seem somewhat shuffling and evasive. By comparison with the focussed clarity available to the Faithed, it is, in a way. But such a comparison is false. The Faithed and the Ungifted are in this respect as different as night and day. Literally: for with the privilege of their gift, the Faithed are apparently able to look upon the objects of their belief with the same sort of directness with which one sees things in daylight. But what happens when such privileged light is not available? At night, the eye strains and hovers, borrowing help from every available source of glimmer; and what it would see, it must see obliquely—because one of the curiosities of night-time vision is that objects disappear when they are looked at directly. One may focus directly on direct sources of light, but when it comes to making out the darkling presences which those glimmers illuminate so gently and suggestively, it turns out that grasping them out of the corner of the eye is the best one can do.

So it is with the faith of the Ungifted. What may to the Faithed seem to be a disappointing feebleness is actually, from the inside, experienced as a strength: for it includes a power of suggestion and affirmation that leads beyond the objects to which it particularly attaches into a vision that includes but transcends them. Of course, belief all by itself has no capacity to rise beyond what it definitely establishes to what it can only suggest and point toward. That is why, in a theological tradition that has (quite understandably) been dominated by the Faithed, the oblique Christianization of the Ungifted may seem a bit strained and contrived. The Faithed are used to going it on faith alone. Whatever does not work with that kind of clarity may

108

appear by comparison rather wishy-washy—though I suspect that the Faithed have generally been more understanding than their imitators, the hidden Ungifted who protect themselves by muffling their minds within a hard-line orthodoxy. But that is one of the important limitations of a religious tradition dominated by the Faithed. Theirs is not the only way, bright as their guidance may be. In the more twilight regions of human religious understanding, the Ungifted have discovered and preserved their own secrets concerning the ways in which the human spirit is nourished and brought into the effective presence of the mysteries that make us free. Faith is only one way, and although it is not entirely closed to the Ungifted (who characteristically have faith in, for instance, the Jesus of Faith and Christians of their acquaintance), still it is only in a very limited sense the way they can travel. I want to deal briefly with two others, characteristic of the way of the Ungifted and far more important to the balance of Christian understanding than is ordinarily supposed.

The first is hope. What do you think of when I mention that? My guess is that it comes on more timidly, in more pastel colors, than the faith that has just been the subject of our consideration. And that, I think, is quite wrong—a common but crucial misunderstanding of the way in which we are put together. Faith, in traditional understanding, has commonly invaded the territories of hope and tried to take prisoner all that belongs to it—just as night-vision tends to long for daylight. The mistake is as easy as supposing that real femininity is actually only an enfeebled version of masculinity—as easy and as false. But it haunts us everywhere, demanding of us that we turn into impossible confidence relationships which have a sturdiness of quite another kind, until we begin to feel guilty about what we are. Hope applies to what is not fully present, what is therefore not a real object of confidence. To have faith in what is hidden, in what is future and unborn, in what lies muffled in mystery, is either a great gift of grace or an impossible dream. For those who are not thus gifted or dreamy, these are the fields where hope grows, not faith, and to insist on faith is to abuse our understanding and our self-acceptance. Have *confidence* in yourself, say the well-wishers to the anxious and uncertain; and the latter, seeing more clearly than their friends can what they know themselves to be and where they want to go, are shaken by the impossible demand of believing in what has not yet come to be, does not exist. It is indeed possible to be graced in such a way as to have full confidence about such things. But the normal human condition forbids it unless grace intervenes. To the Ungifted, it simply does not make sense to ask one to be confidently certain about things for which the grounds of certitude are not present. The proper request is for hope, not faith.

What is hope? Basically, it is the affirmation and expectation of what has not yet arrived. Again, not expectation in the more confident sense of the word, the way one expects the sun to rise and the taxes to be levied, but in the bolder and riskier sense: the way one expects that this estrangement is only temporary, that justice will be done, that the truth will prevail. Hope is the way in which our creative imaginations fill out the patterns of the uncompleted world, as we anticipate what may appropriately follow in a world where grace can baffle cynical prediction and offer wonderful surprises and transformations.

Hope is one of the most important ways in which we are held together, and in which the world we know and live in is held together. Hope fails to get proper credit because of the way in which faith has held the spotlight for so long. But there it has been all along, doing its work in the wings while we applaud faith and think of hope as being only a weak imitator. "She really has faith in herself," say the admirers as some courageous woman struggles against great opposition. Nonsense. She probably does have basic faith in herself, but that isn't what takes her where she's going. That's only a starter. What gives her the impetus that makes the difference is that her hope outbids the limits of her faith—that in spite of knowing herself as a very limited person in an overwhelming system, she realizes that things can work out better than they had a right to, that limited people can be more effective than their talents can guarantee, that life is full of gifts and surprises and interesting loopholes, enough to justify taking the chance of being courageous about it. People whose verve is really built on their self-confidence are likely, when they meet with failure, to become bitter and cynical or to fall apart—because, as they see it, justice has not been done to their deserving and the world owes them redress. But those whose vitality is based rather on hope retain a resilience. They do not suppose that they have been cheated when they fail; they have merely not received a gift for which they were potentially eligible but to which they were not really entitled. So they can begin again, keeping quite clear about the difference between justice and grace, unbothered about the sense of their own deserving (because they know that what they deserve does not set the limits on what may be) and undaunted by the fact that their aspirations seem extravagant (because they know that grace can scatter calculated possibility like the wind that bloweth where it will).

One perennial suggestion of the wise is that we ought to accept the world as it is. The one desire which we must abandon, says a Buddhist commentator, is not the desire for food, or pleasure, or honor, or even the desire for wealth: it is simply the desire that things be other than they are. Let all things be reconciled. And yet this is still not quite the whole story, from a Christian viewpoint; and here there is a dividing of the ways between the Buddhist and the Christian. We must accept. There we are in accord. The Buddhist declines to go much farther, because he has withheld from the things he accepts any assent to their utter reality; he accepts them as *seeming* real, but does not suppose that they can claim more than that—and since they then do not really matter, there is no more that need be said. The Christian, on the other hand, has traditionally accepted them on their own terms, not as seemings but as realities open to real changes; they are not only solid and vivid enough to have value, but capable of solid and vivid value-changes. They *do* matter, and what happens to them matters too. So it is not enough to accept them, not even to take them as real: one must include along with this acceptance an invitation to them to become still better than they are. Not a demand; perhaps not even a desire, lest that compromise the acceptance; but at least an invitation.

To relate to the world hopefully is to allow it space to grow in. If that sounds suspiciously as if I am getting confused about who is in charge of it, let me hasten to acknowledge not only that I am quite aware that the world does not generally depend on my permissions but also that in a particular way, it *does:* in an extremely important sense *my* world is largely determined by what I am willing to let it be. As I suggested earlier, if I choose to understand it as nothing but fortuitous combinations of atoms, I confine myself to a weary, stale, flat, and unprofitable world from which nothing but grace can rescue me. I will think that I am accepting all the atoms just as they are, and allowing them the right to shift and recombine as they please. And this would then be true enough; but unless I somehow learn to invite them to be more than mere atoms, my "acceptance" of them is as confining as a parent's "acceptance" of his 10-year-old child that freezes the relationship at the child's age-10 state, and resists according it the changing dignity that the child strives to realize in growing up further. If I do no more than accept, I tend to laminate the world with the mental plastic of my own limited understanding, sealing it against growth. Only if I affirm, in my very act of accepting, the invitation to be still richer and more wonderful, do I allow things to disclose to me, however slowly and gradually, that they are already more than I had taken them to be, that I must grow to meet them where they secretly already are. Only such hope can make us free.

This applies to every relationship. I must—even to be merely *fair* to both myself and the other—always hope that I can learn still more from this experience if I listen still more attentively, that I can be still more impressed with the beauty and dignity of that object if I honor it still more concentratedly, that this person and I may bless one another yet more thoroughly if I refine my understanding and acceptance further—and invitingly. Hope belongs as a creative partner in every way in which I secure and develop my own reality through affirming the realities I encounter. But it is no less important to realize the part that hope plays in our sense of the value and the possibilities of the *whole*. What sort of world is it, all in all? The answer depends in part on the quality of faithfulness and honesty in one's understanding, for it will not do to pretend the non-existence of either suffering or gladness in order to get a congenially comfortable or cynical result. One begins by seeing and accepting what is really there. But beyond mere accuracy, and beyond mere faith, extends another dimension of the answer in the form of hope. Reality is partly defined and understood by the hope with which we affirm and accept it.

There is no virtue in being timid about this. One must, of course, stay clear-headed about where and in what degrees hope may be properly invested. It is not a license to disregard the way things tend to work. It would not do, for instance, to sink all one's hoping energies into an invitation to the stock market to reward the investment of one's life savings, and have no hope

113

left to place in one's own capacity for bouncing back if the market doesn't. Hope must be tempered by (though by no means reduced to) the ways in which we understand the world to behave. This kind of tempering is the right way to be cautious about hope. But not over-all timidity: for to be highly conservative about one's invitation to the world at large is a pointless— and even rather ungenerous—impoverishment of life.

It is, all the same, a maneuver that is fairly typical of our time. Consider, for instance, the fashion of referring to one's most important and valuable moments as "meaningful experiences." Dreadful. The phrase is far too pale, too tentative, too gingerly and insecure to touch the vivid and invigorating solidity that such experiences really ought to, and usually do, have. At the top of the scale, one should hold out for nothing less than what he can shout for joy about. Imagine someone shouting, "I've just had a meaningful experience!" It won't do. The joy is the reality; the timid reduction of it to the level of "meaningful experience" is a betrayal, and signals a failure of hope. Unless one's hopeful engagement with the world is bold enough to allow an honorable place to an inarticulate joy, without making excuses for it or translating it into something tamer, one has simply cheated both world and self out of some of their chances to be marvelous.

Now, the Ungifted are less accomplished at believing than the Faithed are, but they are often—partly for precisely that reason—much better at hoping. To some extent, their hope operates as an equivalent in another order: the unwavering confidence of the Faithed in the resurrection of the body and life everlasting defines the normative faith, but it is not greatly different for the Ungifted to invite this from life with an affirming joy, even if they are unable to be confident that it is already securely on the program. The absence of faith does not mean the absence of the ability to affirm authentically: through their hope, the Ungifted may thus be as positive about Christianity as the Faithed.

Furthermore, although faith and hope carry us to only approximately similar, rather than identical, places, the difference is not such as to give faith the unequivocal advantage. Consider, for example, this common situation: a loved one is in critical condition, with the doctors warning you that his chances for recovery are slim. Some of your friends and acquaintances are likely to indulge in the cheap confidence which people sometimes have the good fortune to acquire (and the bad habit of attempting to comfort each other with) under such circumstances: "He's going to be all right, I just *know* he will!" But you must deal with things less glibly. You don't, in fact, "just know" that everything is going to turn out fine. You know that the odds are high against it. You do not therefore *believe* that he will recover. At most, you believe that he *may* recover, which is all the farther that belief may legitimately take you. But you can go beyond this too, into a clear and steady hope that he will recover: a patient and affirming welcome to the grace that may come. Such hope is less brittle than the friends' belief, which is less aware, and sustains both the one who hopes and his world without falsifying either.

For the Ungifted, the absence of belief need not diminish their Christianity. It puts them outside the circle of those through whom the Church sustains and consolidates its memory of the truths and events that gave it birth and life, and keeps them from exemplifying the fullness of Christian gifts. But the Christianity in which they do not yet believe may nevertheless be embraced by them fully and freely through their creative hope. To do this is to bear important witness to the free responsibility of the people of God, and to acknowledge the freedom of grace: and therefore those Ungifted who elect to pass beyond the relative passivity of loyal undisbelief into an active hoping

115

affirmation become an important new way for the Church to know itself and its Lord, and an important embodiment of the dynamics of hopeful life within the Church.

We are not entirely free. I cannot choose what has been my home or my native language or my people. These were given to me before choice was possible. But, having passed beyond the ways and things of a child, I am now free to adopt a people that was not mine, to learn for myself a new language, to create for myself a home. And as I look through past and present, through other cultures and times and places, through the persons and the happenings around me—as I search and ask myself what might be the most fruitfully creative home for me, I discover that for all its difficulties and frustrations and puzzlements and backwardness, Christianity remains for me the best place and way and scope to live in, the richest home my hope can legitimately secure for me.

For Christianity is not only a religious life which can be entered and lived through hope: it is itself a way of hoping about the world. It pushes back the boundaries, raises the stakes, makes room for wonderful surprises, and finally establishes the world we live in as one worthy of our love and justifying of our joy. Christianity is a bold and daring way to hope about life. It fills in the blank spaces of our understanding with audacious proposals, invites God to supply us with favors that the world does not seem ready to offer on its own, and accommodates our most extravagant longings. Timid spirits may feel uncomfortable about hoping that largely. They may find it greedy, or even suppose that people simply can't do it, can't honestly arrive at a steady hope of such dimensions. To the first charge, I plead entirely guilty. It *is* greedy. But since it is a hope and not a demand, nothing less will really do. A hope that does not encompass all my needs and longings and spiritual ambitions would be a defrauding of myself, pointlessly; the only fully honest way to hope is greedily.

The other charge is trickier. It expresses an honest and important misgiving, the fear that there may be a radical self-deception involved in adopting a hope that one recognizes to be rather audacious. Indeed, if hope had to go it alone, this would probably be a crippling objection; but hope is not alone. I mentioned some pages back that I wanted to deal with two ways, besides faith, in which we are sustained and brought into relation with the truth that makes us free. One was hope; the other, to which I turn now, is love.

Although the important place of hope in Christian life and in the Christian church has been generally misunderstood and inadequately valued, love has been more adequately appreciated. Nevertheless, even in this case the subject gets fuzzy very quickly. The traditional celebrations of love, including that of St. Paul to the Corinthians, have done far more for establishing that we hold it in very high esteem than for clearing and focussing our minds about what it really is and how it works. It is uncomfortably easy, for instance, for "God is Love" to get itself understood as meaning approximately "Affection is divine," or for "Love one another" to suggest only "Be fond of one another." One of the most neglected sides of the mystery of love is just the one that makes the most difference in the present business: the role of love in the construction of reality.

The very notion may seem odd. We are so used to thinking of reality as a finished given, to which it is our part simply to submit and accept, that it is sometimes difficult to realize that it is nothing of the sort. We are directly given only, at most, the raw materials. We receive them under the guidance of our culture's habits of organizing them. Accordingly, cultures develop both similarities and differences not only in the distribution of values of various kinds—what is beautiful, what is good, what is edible, what is precious, even what is especially conducive to happiness—but even in the ways in which the "facts" are formed: one culture considers all plants and stones to be full of life and power; another refuses to make any substantial distinction between what happens in dreams and what happens in waking history; another maintains that the sun is not the only star that exerts an important influence on crops and dispositions. And although there are tendencies, when cultures interact with one another, to weed out the less successful modes of "realizing" the world in favor of the more fruitful or efficient or coherent ones, the differences in the constituting of reality are not simply differences in degrees of sophistication or civilization. Our culture has long since, and on the basis of good evidence, learned to distinguish sharply between dreams and historical events—but there remains very considerable dispute among various schools of psychology about just what sort of reality dreams are, and what their meaningful or valuable properties may be. Civilized sophistication helps to refine and perfect the sense of reality, but does not solve all its puzzles. It sometimes causes new difficulties: I have earlier issued my complaint that the most technologically and scientifically advanced society is also the one whose sense of reality is in some ways most humanly impoverished.

In some respects, our freedom in the constituting of reality is highly limited. We may see blue as quite like green or as quite different from it; but we are not at liberty to see it as virtually indistinguishable from marmalade, or as the opposite of middle C. But in other ranges of reality, our participation is much more active and our freedom much greater: we can take moral ideas with great seriousness or dismiss them almost altogether; we can consider people to be bothersome things or holy presences; we may have some choice about whether the world we formulate for and represent to ourselves is or is not furnished with friends, saints, ghosts, villains, invisible elves, progressiveness, dignity, astrological determinism, or grace. These choices are guided and strongly influenced by our cultural context and its habits, but we are not entirely imprisoned in the surrounding culture. We retain an independent knowledge and belief, an independent imagination with which to explore possible worlds, an independent capacity for hope through which we may shape the living-space of the world that embraces us. We have some options about settling down in what finally appears to our considered reflection the best and worthiest place to live.

And beyond these powers, we also have one more enormously forceful capacity for forming our world: the ability to love. This operates in many obvious ways, influencing finally whom I marry and whom I seek out as friends, and strongly conditioning how satisfied I shall be with my work, my town, even myself. But it also works in other ways, more subtle and elusive but as crucial.

In the first place, it affects the character of the things we deal with. The difference between a souvenir and an old thing is basically a difference in the way the imagination defines reality: the souvenir is an old thing which has been allowed to be reminiscent of, and therefore to speak about, places or persons or events outside itself. But through the agency of love, a further transformation is possible: the souvenir may become a keepsake—not only remembering but embodying, not merely speaking about but manifesting. The investment of love changes natures, meanings, powers: it transforms Someone to Beloved (or even to Friend), Something to Treasure, Someplace to Home.

In the second place, it affects the characters of ourselves. As we live and move among things and persons thus changed, we too change to meet them. Enriched by the presence of friend, treasure, home, we find ourselves in a world whose values decay

119

far less quickly than they once did: they are stabilized and conserved by our love, and we are accordingly stabilized and conserved through our relationship to them. And to ourselves: for it is only love turned inward that can rescue us from the wastefulness and spiritual destitution of self-contempt into the self-forgiveness and self-acceptance that brings dignity and steadiness, permitting value to gather and accumulate in one's life rather than being progressively amputated in a series of self-rejections.

Love can reach and activate the hidden and secret potentialities of things and persons. In so releasing and enlarging them, it changes the world and, along with the world, those who dwell in it. But it is not confined to those mysteries which are concealed within the contemporaneous and visible. It may attach to things unseen and dreams not yet realized—as the revolutionary leader may be sustained by a love for the long-dead hero Simon Bolivar, the unhistorical Hector, and his future people as he envisions them in their prosperous peace. Now: whatever is so loved begins to emerge into effective reality, whether or not it was there before. The fictional character begins to come alive in someone's historical truth; the abstract ideal begins to be concretized and realized. The dead begin to be raised: the word becomes flesh.

It is here that I think one finds the answer to the objection I entertained a few pages back—that is, that it is impossible for the Ungifted to hope honestly in what they recognize as an almost impudent extreme. Were they dependent on hope alone, the objection might prove fatal. The bold claims and promises of Christianity might make them lose heart and drive them back to more modest aspirations. But if they love the Christian good news, cherishing it for what it has whispered to them from time to time, and for what it has made of others whom they love (whether in this time or earlier ages), and for what an

amazing life it invites us to consider ourselves summoned to—
then the impudence fades, the staggering grandeur no longer
seems so unthinkable, the courage to hope comes easier. What
I manage to love is thus given membership in my world, is made
real in a way that already touches me; in a way, it is even
brought to belong to me—or at least I am brought to belong
to it. I am free to love what I do not yet believe, be it an
intriguing insight that I have not yet tested, or the image of my
future consummately sane and peaceful self, or Christ the Lord
of heaven and earth. We are then drawn together into being
(whether I am made real in its world or it in mine does not
matter—it may in fact be both). I am changed, re-formed in
the image and likeness of the mystery I have loved: the word
is made flesh, and enters really and factually into the history of
my life. This may be the first step in the way to believing, or
may be the first step in another way that makes believing unnecessary. But that doesn't matter either.

What matters is what, either way, is created. I and my world
are created together, bit by bit, formed in the image and likeness of what I have seen and loved in you and in your world
and in all the worlds of good news given me by my own imagination and by the most reverently preserved remembrances of
past revelation. For I know that my world and I are constantly
being created by the power of what and whom I love, and I
know therefore that I must love whoever and whatever will
create us most worthily. Not what is commonly loved, or easiest,
or most readily congenial to what I have so far managed to
become, but what is capable of creating the best and realest
world my imagination can reach or my attentiveness remember.

The Christian belonging of the Ungifted is sturdily founded on
what we really believe, and what we discover to be really relevant to us. But this is only the bedrock on which we build, not
the whole authentication of our Christianity. What counts far

more in our case, whether or not it applies also to the Faithed, is what our hope and love bring for us from there on. We must reach into future and past alike—it would be unfaithful to our capacity to hope if we were to reduce what shall be our home to what has already been our home; but it would be unfaithful to our capacity for love if we did not try to preserve the life of where we have been to help nourish where we now elect to go. And thus, striving both to conserve and to create, the Ungifted build their Christianity in hope and in love—whether toward faith or beyond faith, I know not, God knows—because they perceive this to be the greatest world they know how to dare. It is not for the timid; and to those whose spirits falter at such a staggering project and whose misgivings tempt them to suppose that it cannot really and honestly be accomplished, I give one last parable, in the form of a sonnet Englished from a poem by Rainer Maria Rilke (1875–1926, German or Austrian poet and sometimes writer, born in Prague)—and he who has ears to hear, let him hear:

> This is the creature that they could not know,
> That was not. Still: the whiteness of its neck,
> Its carriage, and the turnings of its quick
> Step, and its brightening glance:—they loved it so.
> Estranged from Was Not, which its lovers hid,
> It grew just real enough. They cleared a space,
> And in that delicate unpeopled place
> It lifted up its head and almost did
> Not need to be. They fed it, not with food
> But possibility, almost a way
> Of being. It grew slowly strong; it stood,
> And grew one horn. Then, delicate as they
> Had dreamed, stole towards a maid as if it were—
> And was: in her silver mirror, and in her.

VIII

"I can't face the Cabinet tomorrow," said Ahab. "It's going to be a nightmare."

"What are you talking about?" asked Jezebel.

"The Assyrian tribute," said Ahab. "I'm going to pay it. There's no way I can avoid it."

"So?" shrugged Jezebel. "When you gotta pay, you gotta pay. What's the big fright?"

"It's going to tear the country apart," said Ahab. "Elijah will blow his stack about paying anything at all; the Treasurer will be furious about paying that much; and the Secretary of the Army, who is scared witless about the possibility of an invasion, is going to scream about taking risks in paying so little. Sometimes I think Moses made a big mistake in guiding us out of the desert."

"You are a sensitive fathead," said Jezebel. "There's nothing to worry about."

"Easy for you to say," said Ahab, "but it's my country, baby, and I'm not looking forward to watching it fall apart from internal dissension."

"It may be your country, sweetie," said Jezebel wryly, "but you understand it about as well as moles understand astronomy. You don't even know who you can count on."

"I know what I can count on," said Ahab. "A furor tomorrow that we might never recover from."

"What a crybaby," sniffed Jezebel. "You get so shaken up if anybody raises his voice that you don't stop to see what's going

on. *Elijah will make a terrible scene, but there isn't a more loyal man in Israel. He just has to let you know how he feels, that's all. The same with the others. They'll yell their heads off about how stupid they think you're being, but they'll back you up as solid as the Lebanon."*

"Well, maybe you're right," said Ahab. "But the disunity bothers me all the same. I just wish we could all agree for once."

"Don't be so childish," said Jezebel. "You don't know what disunity is, for heaven's sake. It isn't a matter of whether you agree, it's how you handle your disagreements. You and I have seen eye to eye about four times since we were married, but we never thought of walking out on each other."

"Well . . . true," said Ahab, "but that's different. We love each other."

"What's what isn't different," said Jezebel. "That's why your cabinet isn't going to walk out. Even if some of them get almost as sharp-tongued as your darling wife. They have to say where they stand, and they hope you'll be convinced by them. But they don't have to say that they trust you anyway, and so they probably won't say it, even though it's true. Any more than you'll give Elijah the satisfaction of letting him know that his crusty stubbornness helps give you courage."

"How did you know that?" said Ahab. "I never mentioned it."

"I watched you, for one thing," said Jezebel. "And for another, he affects me that way too—but if you ever tell him that, I'll scratch your eyes out."

The Gathering

IT would have been perfectly natural for the earliest Christians to have called themselves a synagogue. But instead of using this current and ordinary term for a religious assembly, they looked back to an ancient and venerable alternative: they chose the word that was used to describe the assembly of faithful Israelites in the days of Moses, the *qahal*, which translated into Greek (and, later, Latin too) as *ecclesia*. It was a word rich with holy resonances, full of history and hope. A happy choice.

When room had to be made in the English language for some sort of equivalent, we didn't do badly either. The Old Testament reverberations of the original name didn't mean as much in Great Britain as they had done in the Holy Land, so English borrowed its word from another Greek term, *kuriakon*, meaning "belonging to the Lord." Hence the origin of the Scottish *kirk*, and of the English *church*: it is a beautifully appropriate word, gracefully designating that which belongs to the Lord; it is a frank, sturdy, four-square Anglo-Saxon word, tough and enduring as an oaken staff. It is an excellent word—but I cringe slightly every time I use it.

My problem with it, which you may or may not share, is that I can't say with it what I want to say. I try to get my focus straight, I remember where it comes from and how it applies to that which is called into being by the divine invitation to life in the Lord—but then, when I try to mean that in using the word, I suddenly find that all sorts of other things that belong to the same word start creeping in where I don't want them.

There is the building, to begin with. If there is anything that I don't want to mean by *church,* it is a pompous, pretentious, uncomfortable, humorless marble mausoleum: but when I use the word, I find that images of that sort of church come skulking around at the edges of my attention, no matter how I try to sweep them out. And then there is the sense of the word that crops up in a usage like "Holy Mother Church," a phrase which quietly assures us not only that the Church knows best and will take proper care of us if we are obedient, but also that, whatever else the Church may be, it is not we ourselves. Rather some important, distant, and superhumanly wise Other, based (at least in my tradition) in Rome, but with authoritative outposts throughout the world. I don't want to mean that either when I say *church,* because I want it to be all of us together who are called in Christ; but I find it creeping in all the same. This is the more unfortunate in that my associations with this sense of the word are not even very maternal, on the whole. Holy Stepmother Church, maybe. Or at still more uncomfortable moments, the sense gets even more restricted, pointing to a powerful and unresponsive ecclesiastical government, loftily removed from sight and with a slightly sinister air of secrecy. The Vatigon.

I don't want to mean those things. What I want to point to is the people of God, those who hear and answer the call that brings them together in the presence of the Lord and gives them a new life of health and healing. "Church" is just too tainted with other associations for it to be able to accomplish this meaning for me. And therefore, in an attempt to get closer to the thoughts I am pursuing, I shall no longer speak of the church: I shall speak rather of the Gathering.

The Gathering is, in the first place, those who have gathered —the assembly that responds to the call, like the Israelites in the desert and the people of the highways and byways who have accepted the unexpected invitation to the wedding feast. It is also those who have *been* gathered, through the Lord's way of bringing them together and to himself. It is as small and particular as the group that gathers this week in that place to worship together; it is as large and universal as all those who have ever been gathered into the mercy of God. Moreover, the Gathering is what they are all about: they participate in the work of gathering themselves, each other, and whatever permits itself to be saved, into the house of the Lord. The Gathering cannot possibly be misunderstood as a place or a government or a mysterious group of Others: it is ourselves and our chosen way of life, and all those with whom we belong because of it.

All those with whom we belong; perhaps even *to* whom we belong. For one of the most amazing things about the Gathering lies in the way its members relate to one another. I am not referring to their having benevolent attitudes to one another. I am not even talking about their making commitments to one another. I speak rather of some far more mysterious and remarkable happenings which, when the Gathering is at its best, break down the barriers of isolation altogether and create a unity that is much greater than mere agreement, greater even than mutual acceptance.

One of these mysteries is the shared secret. A common sort of mystery, to be sure, since everyone, I suppose, has experienced the wonderful sense of mutual belonging that comes about among the members of a group that is in on a secret together. Most shared secrets get a good deal of their power to unify from their power to exclude: *we* are brought together because we have created, by our secret, a *they* who are kept out. But the secret which the Gathering keeps, it keeps publicly, excluding no one who really wants to be in on it: it is the good news and the life that it brings with it. It is one of the most public secrets in the history of the world, but it remains something of a secret because no one can quite know what it is until he has tried living it. That is what the Gathering is about. Its members are in on a discovery so full and astonishing that it absorbs everything they are and dwarfs everything else they know: they are in on the invitation to divine life. Even they are not able to realize all the time what that means. But when they do, small wonder that they see one another in a special light, as fellow-sharers in something so amazing that it makes their differences and disagreements trivial and binds them together beyond all power to divide. It is a secret in which they long to include everyone; but until everyone is ready to accept it, it must remain partially opaque to all but those within the Gathering. And they, knowing what their fellow-members too realize, knowing that they too have been gathered to the presence of God, can smile at one another the smile of the secret-sharer, and meet in a mystery of mutual belonging that is to them deeper than death.

Another of the ways in which the Gathering is bound together is through participation in one another. This too is an ordinary occurrence, at least in its simpler forms; but though it happens commonly, it often goes unappreciated, and therefore undeveloped—like a talent that peeps out through the ordinary behavior of its possessor but never falls under the glance of someone who would recognize its significance. Even the Gathering has not learned to exploit its powers of participation very fully, or to realize what great riches are hinted at in some of our ordinary routine responses. For instance:

Suppose I meet a good friend of yours at a party and fall into conversation about this book; and that I, taken with her immediately because she reminds me of someone I am very fond of, am further charmed by the gentle candor with which she speaks of what dissatisfied her, and the perceptiveness with which she had evidently understood what I was trying to accomplish. Then suppose that, as we are falling into spirited agreement about the merits of her favorite religious writer, we are silently joined by a friend of mine, unknown to her, who has occasionally in the past assured me—at length and with obvious feeling—of his total contempt for the same writer. Suddenly my reactions change. I wish he would go away, or at least say something; but he doesn't—he stands expressionless as she is recounting with verve her first experience with this writer (which I perceive with pleasure was very like my own). Before she finishes her story, someone calls to her, and she excuses herself and departs. I feel a bit disappointed; yet a bit relieved. I turn to my friend with rather mixed feelings—slight annoyance, slight embarrass-ment, the afterglow of recent delight—and begin with an affec-tionate (but also somewhat pointed) reference to his absent and more sympathetic wife: "Isn't it too bad Jenny couldn't come—the two of them would have got on marvelously!"

This is a fairly common sort of experience, which I presume you have paralleled often in your own life. But it is a highly intricate one, all the same. Notice what happened. I started the conversation in a highly positive and receptive frame of mind, but before it was over I was having rather complicated reactions. Why? Because I grew with the conversation. When it was just the two of us, it was unqualifiedly comfortable. But when my friend sidled over, I started hearing your friend not only with my own ears (which were delighted) but with his as well (which were not). Automatically, I had expanded to include him within my own consciousness, distributing my presence into his to the extent that I became partly him. And why did I feel slightly embarrassed? Because I had been doing the same thing with her: I was lending myself to her, participating in her, to such an extent that I was somehow feeling some responsibility for what she was saying—as if I were saying it in her, and doing so even though I knew I was making my friend grit his teeth.

And then the reference to the absent Jenny. How did this arise? Because of the fact that I had been receiving your friend through my capacity to share in Jenny too. Having noticed early in the conversation that the two of them had a great deal in common, I was adding to my enjoyment by experiencing your friend as a Jennyized version of myself, as well as directly. I was, over this brief adventure, four different people in varying degrees— myself plus three others whom I brought into presence within me through sympathetic participation.

We all do that. It is a remarkable achievement, with far-reaching implications; but it is very ordinary. Significantly, the fact that the four selves in the hypothetical example are not entirely in agreement with one another does not prevent them from living together in me. It might not even make me any more uncomfortable for them to jar a little if I were a little more mature; for I was accepting and affirming each one, just as I understood each to be, on his (and her) own terms—and though it may be vaguely inconvenient to embody such disagreements, reconciliation lies there and not in the elimination of differences. I was caught off balance. In a more poised and generous moment, I would not have been bothered. When I learn to extend my participation more broadly, of course, and to embrace more deep and serious collisions of interest and value, then there will be greater pain involved in being all those whom my sympathy enlarges me to be. But even then it is the tolerable pain that belongs to reconciliation and atonement, and should probably be expected and welcomed by all those who have been at least initiated into the wisdom of Christ.

Now, the pretended case was a casual one—an ordinary party, a situation with no particular intensity, a rather relaxed experience. All the same, even in such a low-key moment, one's versatility for participation in other persons is quite high. Not because we try; it happens quite inadvertently and automatically, as if we couldn't help extending ourselves. If it works in that way when it doesn't much count and we aren't really trying, think of what it could be if we really put ourselves out and struggled, as an act of love, to participate as fully and generously as our spirits could take us.

That is the way of the Gathering. That is another of the secrets of its unity: not that its members believe exactly the same or think exactly the same or even hope exactly the same— but that, in spite of all the differences that exist among them, they love and accept one another. When this is done well, they affirm one another so solidly and loyally that they *become* one another, each more or less able to experience life as each other experiences it. And as each becomes all, receiving and reflecting all in himself, the Gathering approaches the realizing of one of its greatest secrets: its capacity to be, in all its multiplicity, a single inexhaustible person—its destiny to concretize a second time, and even more grandly, the body and the mind of Christ.

This is, of course, a further entry for the participation of the Ungifted in the faith of the Gathering. Faith enters the Gathering itself through those who are its agents and organs: the willingness of the Ungifted to have that faith define the official self-understanding of the Gathering, along with their willingness to be joined to the Gathering that is so defined, initially makes them sharers in the Gathering's faith. But more: to the extent that they also participate directly through accepting and affirming love in the lives of the Faithed, the Ungifted have another way of participating in belief, even—more or less— *experiencing* it. Within the Gathering, love is a way of appropriating the life of the beloved, of enlarging oneself to be him as well as oneself. And when it is turned to God and, in God, to others, love is the Way toward becoming the body of Christ.

The traffic, however, is not one-way. Another of the principles of the Gathering is that no one is excluded, no person should be left ungathered by the body or allowed to omit his contribution from it. It is for this reason that the reception of another person into the Gathering is properly a communal act. Not that the community meets only to approve or disapprove the application, as if it were a finished and self-contained body that wants merely to ensure that its boat will go unrocked and its character quite unchanged. Quite the contrary. Each new member necessarily changes the Gathering, at least so long as the Gathering remains alive and faithful to itself. The community receives the new applicant as an acknowledgement of its willingness to change for the accommodation of its new member; the reception should be communal in order to give the community a chance to make its pledge in the spiritual marriage between it and its new member—for henceforward, for better and for worse, for richer and for poorer, they are all gathered together until death.

It is through the participation that brings such mutuality that the Faithed are able to impress something of the character of their belief not only on the official self-understanding of the Gathering but even on the minds of the Ungifted. But they are not the only ones who are so respectfully received. The participatory mutuality of the Gathering, no matter how inadequately or raggedly or clumsily this may actually be accomplished at first, requires that every member of the Gathering must be so valued and so cherished by the community as to be able to make a contribution to its self-awareness that is unique and fully his.

The Gathering cannot afford to presume that it knows where grace is especially given. It cannot afford *not* to presume that each of its members is graced. This is one of the most important sources of the mutuality with which the members of the Gathering must pursue their self-understanding. The public secret that brings them together and sets them on a Way and a Truth and a Life together is an important and indispensable start; but as long as the Life is not finished, the Way not yet fully traveled, there remain dimensions of the Truth not yet elaborated, not yet realized, not yet even discovered. Where shall they be found? The traditional answers to this question must still be attended to carefully: search the Scriptures, deduce more exactingly from the present understanding, listen to the certified wise and the authoritative. But because we cannot know for sure where grace is especially given, we cannot assume that the portion of the public secret that still remains private is hidden only in Scripture, or only in undiscovered logical implications, or in the scholars or authorities. For how did we know where to start in the first place? How did we recognize, to begin with, that revelation which we are trying to enlarge and deepen? We must start in what must be for us at first the ultimate place: that totality and depth of our own selves in which spirit may speak and be acknowledged. All our capacity to recognize Scripture, or authority, or wisdom derives ultimately from this home of grace within us, where we receive and welcome truth in a way that may change and grow as we change and grow but over which nothing—not life nor death nor angels nor powers nor any other created thing—can triumph.

Where is the secret buried? I think that the most plausible answer is that it is buried precisely there where it is partially but steadily revealed: in the still-undisclosed mystery of our persons. As we slowly emerge from our hiddenness, rising to meet each other and our world and the Lord of both, we bring into the reach of our own understanding, and of the understanding of the Gathering that embraces and shares in us, the revelation of ourselves and of that manifestation of truth which we incarnate. This has always been God's most important and persistent way of revealing himself; for once the visions and thunderings and cascades of fire from heaven have receded into

133

the distant and doubtful past, what can separate the Lord who spoke through them from the bugbears and bogeymen of our ancestors' inventive imaginations? Many things, perhaps; but one of the most important—and to my mind, the main and indispensable one—is the way in which his story and his invitations echo in the spirit of him who I most truly am, and the way in which your voice echoes there too when you tell me of these things.

He shows himself to us through each other. Through prophets and visionaries, in more spectacular moments, but not them alone, or always. What I perceive of him—through several glasses, very very darkly—owes something to the work of Moses, and to the testimony of Elijah, and to the writings of Isaiah; it owes immeasurably more to Jesus, without whom I would probably never even have known about Moses, Elijah, and Isaiah; but its immediate growth was inspired and nourished by persons who were rather more ordinary, but whose presence to me spoke a good news in a more vivid and living way than even the stories of the holy heroes could do. Many of them would be surprised to realize that they had meant this to me. They would suppose it a great and unanticipated grace that such important disclosures could take place through the revelation of their ordinary and unsaintly selves. But they would also realize, if they have been attentive to their own experiences, that it is not so unusual, for all that. For not only were they also gently ushered into the presence of God by the revelation of just such others as themselves: they also know, probably with the same amused wonder that I experience, that God is manifested to them even through their gradual discovery of—of all things—their own poor selves. Even there he has not disdained to make his presence felt and known.

And so he lives within the Gathering, intimately and forever, the secret of the life he is and offers being partly shown among us and partly hidden within. Because he is present and revealed among us, we gather to celebrate and love and participate in the Lord who is thus known and those in whom and by whom he is known. Because he is hidden and concealed among us, we gather to celebrate and love and participate in each other, so that we may be revealed—and, in us, he himself. It is in living this out that we come to realize that the Gathering is a body into which the Lord has incorporated his presence: it is the body of Christ.

As you may have surmised by now, that is what I think "this 'in Christ' bit really means." We love one another "in Christ" because that is where we are: it is the way of loving more accurately and honestly, not less. Far from excluding loving people "as they are," or encouraging us to tamper with their diversified and idiosyncratic selves, this should make it clear to us that we must love them precisely as they are. It is, after all, in who they are (and not in some idealized and general model of what we, in less generous and adaptable moments, might prefer them to become instead) that they must properly be revealed—and with them, whatever they have incarnated. I do not mean to carp at the author of the verse-prayer to which I am once more alluding. It is understandable that he glances only suspiciously at the tradition of thought that speaks of loving "in Christ." That tradition has a long and unhappy alliance with an unhealthy self-contempt that often passes readily for authentic humility, according to which I should regard everything that is really *me* as a deformation and a serious impediment to becoming something better. There is a grain of truth in that, of course; I occasionally suspect—and it is sometimes hinted to me by others, in moments of uncharitable candor—that there isn't much of my present condition that deserves to be salvaged in the long run. Easy enough, from time to time, to understand how St. Paul could cry out with relief as well as joy that "it is not I that live any more, but Christ that lives in me!" But that is, I think, in reasonably healthy folk, not a usual condition—nor is it quite the way Paul meant his remark to be taken. And therefore, if we sometimes find ourselves saying resentfully, perhaps even defiantly, "it darn well *is* I that live," we should be a little clearer about what is being affirmed, and what is not.

Charity may not necessarily begin at home, but it had better arrive there eventually. The commandment to love one's neighbor as oneself is admittedly much more easily fulfilled if you can begin by thinking that you are thoroughly shabby and contemptible, and are therefore free to hold a similar estimation of your neighbor. But that is not, I believe, the way the thing is supposed to work. You are to love yourself. Just as you are. Not so much, or in such a way, as to fix yourself permanently in your present condition, arresting your growth and development on the implicit assumption that any change must necessarily be for the worse. You must, after all, accept yourself with hope, and allow yourself the same growing room as you ought to allow others; you may even hope for particular directions and types of development in yourself, just as you may do for others even in the act of accepting them (though in both cases, you must stay ready to revise, on further consideration, your opinion that your hope was really pointing in the right direction). Because we are alive, it would be a deadly restriction if our acceptance of ourselves and each other were confined to the present moment alone. No, the love must be invested not in *what* this person is, but in *who* he is: and that includes not only his present condition, but also the interesting bundle of future possibilities with which his present condition endows his freedom. To love *only what* we are is a betrayal; but to love *at least who* we are is a necessity.

This does not mean approving of everything. To accept is not necessarily to approve; love itself is not necessarily approval. In my love and affirmation of myself and of others, I reserve the right to mean "*good*—so far, but with some decidedly preferred ways of moving on from here." In some cases, I may be perfectly confident that certain ways I prefer, and therefore hope, would be considerable improvements: the beloved Who becoming a still more readily affirmable What. In other cases, the shape of my hope will be more provisional and uncertain, more readily aware that another kind of development may prove better. I can see, for instance, that a fairly literal imitation of Jesus might indeed be the best course for me to undertake, though according to the assessment of my present degree of self-understanding, that is not what I seem to be suited for— nor an imitation of St. John of the Cross, either, though his alternative to the literal imitation of Jesus is one which I admire. I also admire the alternative of St. Thomas More, whose life was quite unlike the life of Jesus and quite unlike that of St. John of the Cross—and also quite unlike what mine is likely to turn out to be. No matter. Wholesale imitation, I suspect, is simply not the right way of going about Christian living. From those who have shown the way, I intend to borrow this and copy that, incorporating whatever seems to work or make sense in me—just as my tastes and interests have grown and been refined through my participations in other congenial persons. But I am, like you, a new and partially unprecedented Christian experiment, and the way it is to be conducted is not by the choice of this model or that, but through a new creation. Christ lives in me only to the extent that I myself come alive. But again, although my Christian experiment and yours may depend on the development of those unique centers of human vitality that are the essential me and the essential you, still we are not confined to just that: we become enlarged by participation in others, and by participation in the presence of God, to something

137

far grander. And therefore if our experiments turn out to be fairly successful, if we are permitted to outgrow limitations and deficiencies that kept us from realizing our potentialities within the Gathering, and if our participation in its other members grows and develops, then I think we may be excused if, astonished at having become revealing and unique facets of the many-splendored body of Christ, we cry out with joy, "I am not the man I used to be, and now Christ shows his life in me too!"

Now, some of the Ungifted would undoubtedly have difficulty putting it that way. Although solidly affirming of the Jesus of Faith, the Ungifted may have far less security about the Christ of History. How, they may wonder uneasily, can I follow the leap from Jesus of Nazareth to the cosmic and glorified Christ who is said to be working in us, transforming us? How can I really claim that Christ lives in me, when I barely know what it means to say that Christ lives at all—and even that little understanding is on loan from the Faithed? The answer is that such a one can follow such a leap only indirectly, through participation in the Faithed. But for himself, he cannot follow. At least not by the same route, since that path requires that he see what can be grasped only by the faith that he does not have: namely, the total continuity between Jesus of Nazareth and the Christ of History. But there is another way in which he may proceed. He does not see the continuity; but he does see both sides. Let him call the one the Jesus of Faith, and call the other by the name of Christ. The Gathering is, according to traditional theology, the Body of Christ—Christ-in-history, continuing to act in a new way. The Ungifted can affirm this by starting precisely from that point and saying: this is what I shall mean by the name Christ, the holy power that manifests itself in the Gathering—the Way that it is following and the Life that it lives. I do not yet know how this Christ is related to the Jesus of Faith, though it is at least clear that Jesus stands at its beginning as its founder and origin; I can grasp only very dimly the claim made by the Faithed that Jesus and this Christ are one and the same, living only in different ways. But I can accept that this claim defines the way in which the Gathering must try to understand itself, even though I do not see its truth. For my part, I must wait and listen, straining my eyes into the darkness to see the shape that is mercifully given to the eyes of the Faithed.

In the meantime, though I cannot say what they say or see what they see, I can affirm as a starting point and as a common understanding with the Faithed that this Gathering is the living body of Christ, is Christ-in-history, is—because it strives to be— the Son of God. Beyond that, I must wait to see if I will be shown more of Christ than I now can grasp, more than the life of the Gathering itself. I have not given up on that possibility. I still hope to know the Truth; and if the identity of Jesus and Christ is one of the secrets which the Truth still hides from me (which I am not in a position to be sure is the case, but toward which my participation in the faith of the Gathering turns the attention of my hope), then the same hope invites this to be revealed within my understanding. Until that happens, I must continue to pursue whatever offers itself to me as a hint of truth, whether or not it seems to anyone else to lead in that direction, and hope that even if I am not entirely acceptable as I am, I shall nevertheless be forgiven for it.

I do not mean to imply that the condition of ungiftedness is intrinsically sinful (unless you take sin to mean incompleteness of any kind, which I would consider a dangerous adulteration of the word's force). It is not only sin that needs to be forgiven. Forgiveness applies as well to disappointments, unrealized opportunities, unactualized hopes. Forgiveness, in short, applies to every gap between what is and what might have been, and is one of the other most important sources of strength and unity in the Gathering.

For let's be honest with one another. There are things about me that you can hardly stand. You may realize perfectly well that it isn't entirely my fault that I talk too loud (and often), and you may generously suppose that my taste in clothes might have been quite normal in the place I originally came from, and you may allow that everyone is entitled to form their own honest opinions about politics, even the uninformed. You may realize all this, and tell yourself to let it be—but that really doesn't make it much easier not to be annoyed by my sound, by my appearance, by my conversation. You know that I deserve to be accepted, in spite of everything, but you just don't feel accepting. Well, be comforted. The truth of the matter is that I feel the same way about you. Somehow your eyes remind me of a wretched teacher I had in the early grades, and I've held that against you from the start. Besides, I've never liked your nervous giggle, and have always despised the work of the two artists you're always raving about. Sometimes it is all I can do to be civil to you.

Fortunately, we are not stuck with this mutual alienation—if we have learned how to forgive. And just as charity begins at home, so should pardon: my first step should be to forgive myself for those faults and follies and inadequacies that make it impossible for me yet to be totally delighted with you just as you are. (You, I hope, are busy forgiving yourself for the way you feel about me—and, of course, for the way you *don't* feel about me.) Ideally, we should both have been reflecting on the readiness of God to forgive deficiencies that really can't be helped; but I suspect that the divine forgiveness, though it may be given readily, can be received by us only if we are able to match it with a forgiveness of our own. Which is not easy: we are often hardest on ourselves, and most inclined to punish and withhold pardon from ourselves, presumably because we tend to be most severe with the person who has most thoroughly and bitterly disappointed us. But if we are to receive and experience the pardon of God, we must let go, forgive, accept who we are and what we have been. It is a relieving experience, being forgiven; and forgiving oneself is positively liberating. But not completely. I am now easier on myself, and a little more amused at myself, for my incapacity to receive you happily as you are, but I still have some trouble responding to you. So now must come another act of forgiveness. I must try to realize that I am not entitled to what I want or hope for from you, that I have no right to expect more than you have given me, or anything other than what you have given me—and that you have no obligation to be or do or offer anything else. I must try—but I won't quite make it. I will still find that I want or hope all the same, in spite of knowing that you owe nothing, and I will be disappointed not to have my hopes answered. No use explaining it all to myself any further, it won't help. Until I grow up more, or become more detached, or grow more generous, I will continue to have this small twinge of resentment about you. I have no choice but to forgive you for not being what I had hoped. It seems odd for me to forgive you for what is actually a deficiency in me: but for the time being, that is the best I can do, and we must both put up with it. For better and for worse—and therefore for the borderline between them.

Forgiveness applies to every such gap. It reconciles what I am with what I ought to be, but without reducing the latter to the former or making it seem less important; it reconciles you with me, though without cancelling the need for some

141

further adjustments on both sides; it reconciles the Ungifted with the Faithed, though without eliminating the necessity of further growth in mutuality, which works something like this:

The Faithed are able to recognize that Ungiftedness is not a blameworthy condition. They know that the gift which they themselves enjoy is not theirs by right or even by deserving, but exclusively by the gratuitous mercy of God for the sake of the Gathering. They are aware of all this—but still it is probably difficult for them not to have the sneaking suspicion that their faith is the normal Christian condition, rather than being just the ideally normative one, and that somehow the Ungifted are ungenerously holding back or are being pettily skeptical or lack the courage to make the leap of faith. For their part, the Ungifted know that the confidence of the Faithed is justified within the experience of the gift of faith, and that it is not out of ignorance or naïveté or inexperience that they believe as they do. They know this: and yet, knowing still more vividly that their own integrity leads to uncertainty and qualifies their hopeful assent, they cannot help wondering whether the confident certitude of the Faithed is really a gift or is perhaps instead something stolen, a comfort embezzled from the resources of responsibly critical intelligence. Is it an awakening or a partial falling asleep?—the question will insinuate itself no matter how carefully the Ungifted try to protect their acceptance of the traditional understanding of how faith is given within the Gathering.

Each makes for the other all the allowances that can be made, each meets the other in understanding and sympathy as far as they can. But neither can nor should undo himself in order to enhance his acceptance of the other. There must remain an important dimension within each that takes its stand where he really lives and utters—however provisionally, however tentatively—the judgment of his own integrity: since this cannot be my way, I cannot be totally confident that it is really a thoroughly respectable way at all.

It is therefore at this point that there enters one of the most important acts of forgiveness that can be made by or within the Gathering. The Faithed and the Ungifted must forgive themselves their suspicions of the other and the harsh judgments that they cannot altogether suppress; and they must each forgive the other for not being what their own lives know to be valuable—the Faithed must forgive the Ungifted for not being confident of the holy truths that they know must lie at the center of the Gathering's self-understanding, and the Ungifted must forgive the Faithed for not being still in search of the final truth, for not being as sensitively aware of difficulties and as open to new suggestion as the Ungifted are free to be. And having forgiven themselves and each other thus, the gap between them is closed as far as it can possibly be—almost. There remains only one further step: that each gather the other, through loving participation, into the many-faceted self that each member of the Gathering grows to have. Then they become, beyond all irrepressible suspicions and unavoidable judgments, members of one another: each, at least in one generous division of his versatile self, experiences permanently what it is to know and believe, and what it is to search and hope, with all one's mind and strength. It is only at this level of experience that this can be done. As long as you stay with ideas, knowledge, notions alone, the other must necessarily look suspicious. But when you get to the person himself, then in spite of the gap between his thoughts and yours, you can be in a position finally to say to yourself (even to him): he looks as if he is somehow on the right track, he sounds as if he knows what he's talking about, he seems to be on to something important. The appreciation of the other's position will continue to be mixed with impassioned attempts to get him to change

143

it; but until he shapes up and abandons the ways of his apparently invincible (and rather persuasive) ignorance, he must be valued and accepted.

This has been the way from the beginning. Accepting and valuing one another, despite important differences of view on key religious questions, without belittling or ignoring the significance of those differences, was from earliest times one of the great dignities of Christianity. Consider: during the first Christian generation, the main community in Jerusalem (composed mostly of Jewish Christians) seems to have had a rather conservative attitude toward Christian practice of the Jewish religious law, while the substantially non-Jewish communities in Antioch and in Paul's mission territory had rejected that law. There were frictions and disputes: some of the Jerusalemites came to Antioch, where they disapproved of Peter's custom of dining with Gentile Christians; Peter gave in and withdrew from the Gentile tables, to the great and public annoyance of Paul, who accused him of being inconsistent with the Gospel. Other law-conservatives went among Paul's converts in Galatia and attempted—with some success—to persuade them to keep the commandments of Judaism; Paul objected with fury, and charged the Galatians not to listen to them. There were important issues at stake, and there could be great passion and great bitterness bound up with their working-out, when it seemed to be a question of real infidelity and not just a difference of conscientious opinion.

But honest disagreement did not mean mutual alienation. Early Christianity had its examples of the commonplace showdown; but what is far more significant is that it knew a unity beyond the confrontations of stubborn anger. In the heat of controversies about the law and its application to Gentile Christians, Paul went to Jerusalem to have it out with the leaders there. The situation was potentially explosive: some of the

Jerusalemites did not trust Paul, and thought he was betraying the truth in his failure to Judaize the Gentile converts—while Paul, for his part, stood with adamant and inflexible conviction behind the belief that the Gentiles were free from all claims of Judaism. There might have occurred, on that occasion, a disastrous split in Christianity, proving its inability to transcend its internal disagreements. Paul reports to us what happened instead. The Jerusalem leaders heard him out—and then, seeing that the Pauline mission had indeed apparently borne good fruit, and that Paul's conception of his calling was, for all its untraditional liberalism, evidently that of a man on to something important, they gave him and his partner Barnabas "the right hand of fellowship," and returned them, with their blessing, to the Gentile mission which heaven seemed by these signs to have approved. Gave them the right hand of fellowship! This was an event of staggering importance in the history of the Gathering. Despite disagreements, despite threats to authority, despite the risk to unity that might have been perceived in allowing the Gentiles to go their own un-Jewish way, the leaders of the Gathering were able to see and to trust in the religious integrity of one another. In that gesture of acceptance the Gathering was sealed with a unity far greater than mere uniformity, and was opened to a life that brought its own risks with it but that made growth possible.

The fundamental importance of this aspect of the Christian Way is reflected also in the book that forms its basic constitution: the New Testament. The Christian tradition is used to seeing the diversity of the New Testament as a complex harmony in which every book represents the same understanding of Christianity as every other, only from a slightly different point of view. A lovely conception—but in this case it is simply inaccurate, a wishful thinking born out of a strong bias toward uniformity as the proper basis of unity. No, the New

Testament has the unity not of agreement but of acceptance: the unity of Paul and James and the right hand of fellowship. It is not that the relatively cautious view of Jesus found in Mark merely complements the more extravagant view in John, but that they represent two different and partly inconsistent ways of interpreting Jesus and his work. No amount of attentive reflection is going to make the Christianity of the Epistle of James look essentially like the Christianity of the Epistle to the Galatians. These are two different and disagreeing Christianities, bound together not by coinciding views but by the right hand of fellowship. The New Testament enshrines one of the most important discoveries of the Gathering: its unity is a unity of persons, a unity of love, and its integrity can sustain a lot of unresolved conflicts of understanding without being seriously threatened. Its members may believe in one another enough to be willing to listen to each who seems to know what he's talking about, to entertain his understandings with serious respect even if they conflict with what the listener believes to be true, and to wait for providence to define, in its own good time, the final truth of the Gathering by bringing all its members to see and accept it for themselves. Until then, they must cherish one another, and in this way grow, however slowly, in wisdom and grace.

The members of the Gathering, being especially intent on making room for one another, valuing one another adequately, belonging to one another, will tend to give priority to other members of the Gathering, when it comes to the distribution of their generosity. But it is not for them exclusively. The Gathering, which comes in the name of the Lord, is much more audaciously ambitious than that. It aspires to gather all humanity into itself. It must therefore always be ready to receive anyone who comes, to understand and accept each as far as this is possible, and beyond that to forgive both *what* it does do not understand and *that* it does not understand, both the unaccepted and the unaccepting. And of course the only way that the Gathering can be ready enough to do this is by anticipating their coming. It must affirm and accept the members of other religions too. It must know them as persons graced with a capacity and a thirst for life and truth, persons who have gone a different way but not necessarily astray—persons who even now, before their paths have merged with that of the Gathering of Christ, may belong to a larger and more inclusive Gathering of God whose public secret is partly manifested only in and through them. The Gathering always changes in its absorption of another person. It changes too as it anticipates the absorption of those who have not yet approached it, straining to learn from them already, in accepting affirmation, the secrets about God known to them alone, born of the unique adventure of their own experience.

And so it goes also with the persons separated from us by time as well as those distanced by space and cultural difference. Knowing that God does not abandon that which he has created in love, the spirit of the Gathering knows that nothing that has been blessed by humanity or honored by it as worthy of its attention can fail to be worth appropriating. One of the great strengths of the Catholic tradition in Christianity has been precisely this trust in the dignity and integrity of the past, the conviction that no way of understanding or loving ever becomes quite obsolete, even though it may cease to be fashionable. Through the scholars of the Gathering, the characteristics of the great minds of the past—from the early times of Clement and Augustine down to the more recent times of Newman and Barth—have continued to live and exert their influence on the rich self-understanding of the Gathering itself; and through the ordinary folk of the Gathering, the popular ways of past reverence—from the mistletoe of the Druids and the

147

psalms of the ancient Jewish festivals to the spirituals of the last century and the emblems of the recent peace movement— have been gathered as living ways of rejoicing and giving honor to God. The Gathering knows that nothing which has lived in the Lord needs ever to die altogether. As long as it is possible for man to extend himself, to participate in that which he has not yet become, the past can be as rich a source of enlargement and growth as the divided present. And thus the past too is gathered: all that man is and all that man has been belongs finally to the Lord, and deserves a place in the accumulating life with which the Gathering swells and enriches itself—and by which it practices still more perfectly the living-out of the presence of God. Incorporating what it finds valuable, forgiving and preserving what it does not yet adequately understand, the Gathering lives the more completely by remembering and reawakening whatever has been.

A moment of nasty practicality. This vision cannot be realized. It is the hope of the Gathering, not the actuality. There will always be impediments and inadequacies and blunderings that keep it from coming to be. Just as you and I will never quite make it to the point where we accept and love one another as we both wish and hope to do, so the Gathering at large will never preserve faithfully all that graced humanity has offered to us from the past, or embrace all that graced humanity has made available to us in the present. Can't do it. Our equipment is too shabby, our dedication too incomplete, our faith and hope too inadequate (not to mention our love). We don't seem to be able to melt the standoffish resistance of those fellow-Christians who don't appear to be trying or to care about living the good news—in fact, we're not even very good at melting our *own* resistance. Now: that once admitted, let us turn back to the challenge offered to us by the great and extravagant hope of the Gathering—because even though we are not going to be able to complete this project, there is no way of being excused from it. We must forgive ourselves for being so inadequate to the task, and forgive the world for being so resistant to being gathered, and then get back to work. There is no way of evading the task, because the Gathering is the body of Christ, the way in which the presence of God is made incarnate in human history. Its meaning is to be about its Father's business. Until the love of the Gathering for the world and for its people has reached the extent of the love with which they were created, the work remains unfinished. Until all the knowable secrets of God are recovered, uncovered, discovered by the Gathering, there is more to be done. Until justice prevails universally and the peace of the Lord has triumphed over all opposition, there remains much to do. Because the Gathering is the way God works in the world, the realization and concretization of both his presence and his power, its life will be forever incomplete until all is rescued, all is reconciled, all is made new: until all is gathered into the blessing of the Lord who informs the Gathering and gives it life.

The traditional Christian tendency, when one gets to this stage of reminding ourselves about unfinished business, is to glance nervously at our watches and make pained calculations about how we will have to cut corners, it being this late in the historical day. Settle for 40 cents on the dollar, or concentrate on the Western world only, or manage to scare up, say, ten just men in Sodom, and take the will for the deed as far as the rest of it goes. So we have been doing for nearly two thousand years: for since the time of the resurrection, every Christian generation has been asked to presume that it is likely to be the last, and to mop up its affairs accordingly. The first lot of Christians was quite persuaded that the world would be ended within their lifetimes; and although things have relaxed a bit since then, there is still a reluctance all over the Western

world—and not least within its stronger Christian enclaves—
to plan with more than a couple of generations in view, for
by the time we became capable of imagining that the world
might in fact really go on longer than that, we were already
in the grip of a naïve confidence in the capacity of scientific
technology to take care later of what we could not dream of
dealing with now. Anyway, both versions of this experience
amount to much the same thing humanly: the inability to think
in terms of a project in which basically the same kind of humanity with the same sort of capability would attempt to master a problem over a space of hundreds of thousands—or
hundreds of millions—of years. Oriental religions, accustomed
to thinking of an accumulated past running to billions of relaxed years of remembered events, must generate a bemused
incredulity at the relative frenzy of the West's cramped sense
of time.

But the mood is changing. Suddenly, we are beginning to
project ourselves on a more long-range basis: we calculate the
depletion of natural resources over several centuries, measure
the effects of cosmic radiation into the imaginable future, and
wonder about the possible evolutionary effects of another several millenniums of man. Things are looking up: the time may
yet come when the consciousness of the Gathering, still at this
point intent on managing a holding operation for another
precarious generation, may look to the possible accomplishment
of a systematic advance in the realization of its vital hopes
over a span of time long enough to embark upon a real transformation of the world.

It is, I think, this curiously truncated sense of time that has
made it so difficult for the Christian West to make greater advances toward that new creation which has always haunted its
dreams—and paralyzed its practical imagination. We long for
a world in which all men are free to be wise and good, but

it is so unlike the world in which we live that we surrender the dream to the unimaginable power of God and busy ourselves with patching and stitching up the ragged fabric of our own society. Well: we must still leave hopeful room for the unimaginable power of God, but in the meantime it is irresponsible and unrealistic to fail to recognize and to count on that dimension of the power of God which is not only somewhat imaginable but vividly present—the power of the Gathering, the incarnate presence of God in human history, the body of Christ alive in this world. What this power may accomplish within a couple of years, even given the election of the right political parties (whatever they may be), might appear somewhat doubtful; but over hundreds of thousands of years of devoted effort, the prospects are rather inviting.

Cast your eye back, for instance, over the last couple of millenniums. It is fashionable to react with some impatience to the lack of accomplishment in the history of Christianity. There is no doubt that there has been much laziness, great irresponsibility, huge sins of omission. But on the balance, is the record really so desperate? Without the machinery of the technological revolution, without the availability of vast sums of money to spend on Christian advancement, without even the sense of eager urgency that spurs many modern movements, the messy West has gone in the space of less than twenty centuries from what it was like in the days of the Emperor Nero, when slaves were sold and butchered like cattle and the imperial armies contended with foreign tribes for the world's record in pillaging and murder, to a time when the dignity of individual human lives, the responsibility of mutual care, the possibility of universal community, are well enough established that those who abuse them can no longer safely sneer at these values but must disguise their vandalism under cover of some worthy purpose. We have gone from Britons who dyed themselves blue and followed their priestly Druids in the same sort of human sacrifice that elsewhere repeatedly consecrated the splendid cities of the Aztecs, to a world in which their religious descendents know themselves to be called to generosity and reconciliation and reverence for life. Not bad, for a start. Especially considering what a small proportion of the energies of the West have really been invested in learning what Christianity had to teach, and in living what it had already learned.

I am inclined to believe that the prospects for the next couple of millenniums are not bad. For one thing, Christendom has gradually come to realize that it is something quite apart from the societies and governments of its world, that it has grander aspirations and vaster commitments than they can claim, and a calling that is both more ancient in its inheritance and more ultimate in its destiny. For another, Christians seem now to have a clearer sense than ever before that they are obliged to take responsibility for the hopes which they cherish for the world they love in the name of the Lord as well as in their own. After a long-established tendency to take hope as an invitation to unilateral divine intervention, and as a minor gesture of good will that relieves one of all further obligations, it is now more common to see things in terms of a different moral logic, in which the proper implication of hoping is to act toward the realization of that which is hoped for. Still largely unorganized, still largely unsophisticated in the ways of the world, the modern movements that acknowledge and are faithful to a Christian origin know that they are the way Christ acts, the way God invades and transforms history, and they are coming to know how to go about their Father's business.

In all of this, Christendom ideally acts as one body. Within the Gathering, it matters little whether female or male, richer or poorer, better or worse, Ungifted or Faithed. The Gathering reaches into past and present and future, conserving whatever deserves to live and creating whatever is newly needed in a new moment with new chances and new demands, enacting its way of life so as to embrace and redeem the world. But although there is little point, in the unity of its body, to distinguish between part and part, there may for the sake of perspective be some reason for observing that the history of the Ungifted plays a special part. The Faithed, who have led and formed the Gathering for most of its life, have often been the most active in working to improve the world. But more often, the Faithed are constitutionally inclined to attend with patient expectation the time when the power of God will put all things right. In the dynamics of transformation, whether it be of a single life or of a whole world, the Gathering has probably learned far more from the Ungifted: for it is they who, in their lives and in their dreams, are most experienced in the path that the Gathering faces as its future—the Way and the Life by which hope is, in the mercy and power of God, transformed into Truth.

IX

"I'm awfully sorry, Ahab," said Elijah. "I guess I put you in a pretty awkward position."

"Sorry about what?" asked Ahab.

"The Carmel Caper," said Elijah. "You were sort of put on the spot when nothing happened."

"Hell, no," said Ahab. "You were the one who was on the spot. You may remember that I never expected anything to happen in the first place."

"You bet your horse I remember," said Elijah. "You skeptical bastard."

"If you'll pardon my saying so," said Ahab, "it seems that a little skepticism was in order, as things turned out."

"Touché," said Elijah, "but I will not pardon your saying so."

"So it's no apologies needed, then, either way," said Ahab.

"Okay," said Elijah, "if that's the way you see it. But I can't help feeling a little guilty when I think of the way the people kept looking up at you, waiting for a cue. You had a big responsibility."

"I always have a big responsibility," said Ahab. "And they knew more or less how it would come out. Don't worry about that."

"And I can't help feeling even more guilty when I think of the ribbing you must have taken from Jezebel."

"Right on," said Ahab.

"Sorry about that," said Elijah.

"So," said Ahab, "it's back to work. What are you going to do now?"

"What I've been doing all along," said Elijah. "I'm going to try to get you to come to your senses and pull down all those goddam Baalist shrines."

"Well," said Ahab, "don't hold your breath. As a matter of fact, I'm meeting Jezebel at one of them in half an hour."

"You gutless infidel!" screamed Elijah. "How dare you!"

"Relax, Elijah," said Ahab. "She's my wife, remember? You may be ready to throw her to the dogs, but I happen to be rather fond of her; and if Baal-worship turns her on, then I think there's room in the kingdom for a little of it—and I don't see the harm in my going along with her once in a while. Besides, it's rather interesting. Lively, you know what I mean? We could pick up a few pointers there for the Temple. Some of our liturgy is pretty dry by comparison."

"We?" snorted Elijah. "Our liturgy? Where do you get this we stuff, you heathen liberal? You try tampering with the service of the Lord, and I'll clobber you with your own scepter, so help me."

"Elijah," sighed Ahab, "sometimes I think you must be the narrowest man in Israel. Even Jezebel is the soul of ecumenical understanding, by comparison. I am as loyal a Yahwist as you are, but I just don't see it the way you do. I have to do it my way—and from where I stand, it seems to me that in fact the Baalists have a few insights that we'd do well to learn. I think Yahweh is big enough to allow us to work that way, even if you aren't."

"Ahab," sighed Elijah, "sometimes I think you must be the dullest man in Israel. Even Jezebel understands me better than you do. I have to do it my way too—though I'm pretty damn sure it's Jahweh's way as well—and that includes yelling at you when you're piddling around with this Baalist nonsense. I just *wish the Lord would clear your head up a little. But until he does, I know what you're doing, and I respect it, but I'm going to keep yelling about it all the same. I know that when the Lord wants you to see it my way he'll take care of it."*

"And if he wants you to see it my way?" suggested Ahab, with a smile.

"He'll take care of it," said Elijah. "That's crossed my mind a couple of times. What, I said to myself, if Ahab is really doing the Lord's will in all of this, changing Yahwism the way Yahweh wants it changed, like some sort of secret-service plain-clothes prophet?"

"What if?" smiled Ahab.

"Well, I was pretty mad at first," said Elijah, "but after I thought about it a little more I told him: 'If that's the way you want to work it, you're the boss—but you're going to have some pretty tall explaining to do to old Elijah.'"

The Gathering of the Ungifted

THE Ungifted go home from their unvisited Carmels. There has been no fire from heaven for them—neither the fire that accepts clearly and miraculously the gifts upon their altars nor the fire that falls in tongues upon their heads to bless and inspire them. All the same, it is not as if the failure at Mount Carmel leaves them helpless or despairing. So who expected any action there in the first place? And what is Mount Carmel to them anyway? It was a nice outing, but now we're going home again —and home is the Gathering.

The Gathering is all of us. Not of this time only, for it includes Paul and James; it includes Augustine and St. Francis and Thomas Aquinas and Luther and Schleiermacher; includes the pious craftsmen who made the stained glass windows and carved the votive statues in the great medieval churches, and the pious zealots who shattered them in the early Reformation; includes the courageous unflinching victims of the Inquisition and the devout unflinching Inquisitors. Not of one kind only, for the Ungifted are gathered with the Faithed, the mystic with the revolutionary, the sinner with the saint, and each offers to the Gathering a facet of the Way and of the Life and even of the Truth, without which the Gathering would be less complete, less whole, less perfectly the body of Christ.

The creed which the Gathering as such professes is its memory of who it is and where it has come from. Its Faithed members profess it also as individuals confident of its truth; but even the least of the Ungifted, the confidence of its truth being held from him completely, can profess it as the authentic memory of that venerable body to which he has willingly been gathered, and as the authentic belief of his Faithed and beloved brethren. The prayer and worship of the Gathering as such is the life it has led from the beginning. Its more contemplatively inclined members may live it also as the deepest source of their individual fulfillment; but even the most activist of his fellows, impatient to reorganize and rescue the world, can participate in it as the fountainhead of the mysterious peace and unity of the Gathering, and the place of its most intimate communion with the God to whose presence it offers a body to inhabit and vivify —and as what might turn out to be the source of the greatest power to transform the world.

In times past, that has sometimes seemed to be about as far as the Gathering could go in resolving its differences into unity. The understanding of the Gathering is insufficient; the life of the Gathering is incomplete. What then? It is a normal human condition. The normal response is of two kinds: trying to adapt to the incompleteness and insufficiency by learning to live with it, or trying to resolve them by becoming more sufficient and complete. The two usually go on simultaneously, and often enrich each other. The Gathering has, over its history, probably acquired a more sophisticated experience of adaptation than of progress: its tendency has been to suppose that there is little of importance about itself or its Lord that has not already been disclosed, and that what is needed for the fulfillment of its life is not new developments but a more dedicated and disciplined living out of its traditional Way, as traditionally understood. The differences in behavior and in inclination within the Gathering were thus commonly reduced to unity by the suppression or discouragement of all that did not correspond to the traditional criteria of evaluation. Faith in the over-all system was not much shaken by the emergence from time to time of anomalous results, such as the refusal to treat Jews in a manner befitting human dignity, or complicity in slavery, in political and economic oppression, in the promotion of dehumanizing fear and dependency. Similarly, the differences in understanding and conviction within the Gathering have traditionally been resolved by establishing an official pattern of belief to which every member is expected to conform his understanding; and deviations from this are automatically illegitimate, and are to be quietly suppressed or publicly punished. Here too a sort of unity is achieved; everyone can learn to adapt to the relatively narrow and carefully defined limits of the official orthodox understanding. But the cost is considerable, and possibly disproportionate.

Are the new offerings in living and in understanding so dangerous as they have sometimes been represented? That depends on how much you value uniformity. Wherever free discussion is permitted, there will always be disagreement. If what you want is uniformity, that will not do. Disagreement must be avoided; if it cannot be avoided, it must be suppressed. But suppose that what you want is not necessarily uniformity but rather unity—and suppose that you come to the discovery that there is a way of unity that is greater than uniformity, stronger and richer because more inclusive, a unity that can embrace disagreements without being broken by them. The danger dwindles and shrinks, almost to the point that it needs some resuscitation if it is to be able to bare its fangs or bite ever again. From the standpoint of uniformity, one of the wickedest perversions is Heresy—a name at which virtue trembles and truth gasps. But from the standpoint of unity, it loses its sting: it becomes little more than Eccentricity—a name at which virtue calls upon its patience and truth smiles benignly.

Do not misunderstand me. I am not, not for a moment, saying that error does not matter. I am not pooh-poohing the traditional anxious concern over orthodoxy as an unreal or silly endeavor. If you suspected otherwise, then you have evidently forgotten what I was at pains to insist upon in earlier chapters (or I have been regrettably clumsy in my painful insistence): the traditional conception of orthodoxy matters enormously, and must remain for the foreseeable future one uncompromised basis of Christian self-understanding. Mistaken understanding and mistaken thinking in religious matters can have excruciating and terrible consequences. Many persons have suffered unspeakable agonies through a mistaken conviction that they had committed unpardonable sins; many have perpetrated unspeakable outrages through a mistaken conviction that others had done so. The liberalism of our times makes it relatively easy for us to see that there was important religious error in the thinking that led to the brutal destruction by orthodox Christians of the Cathars and other similar early heretics; but it need not blind us to the forms of cruelty inflicted by the Cathars' hatred of the world and the flesh. Not every misstep in religious thought has serious consequences, of course: some simply render men harmlessly ridiculous. But thinking is a serious matter. In our time, shabby thought has eased the way to the murder of millions of persons by slick governments and efficient regimes. I say eccentricity, not heresy; but even if eccentricity invites virtue's patience and truth's smile at first, they must watch and wait. When eccentricity goes to seed, it can sometimes sow a perilous madness.

But not always. Not even often. Elaborate safeguard systems are unnecessary. A lot of modern thinking, for instance, goes on in universities, most of which are not concerned to be uniform but work according to a principle of unity that is more flexible. One of the consequences is that there is hardly any notion so silly that it has not been solemnly propounded by some university professor. Normally, the offender is neither burnt nor silenced. He is heard out, assessed, and ignored. And

161

although the discussion of various subjects, including religious ones, is often temporarily swayed within the world's academic institutions by various intellectual fads and fashions, on the whole sanity and balance seem to prevail. The whole enterprise would indeed be much more tidy if every subject had a rigorous orthodoxy imposed uniformly on all those who wished to discuss it, but there are two major disadvantages to going about it this way, disadvantages so considerable that it would be disastrous to accept them even in universities—and much more so in the Gathering.

The first is that it is important for those who are still in the process of learning—which is everyone—to be free to formulate what they have learned so far, in the most thorough and accurate way they can, no matter how much it may deviate from official positions. One advantage of doing this is that it makes significant error easier to detect: if I have a sloppy notion that I happen to take for a clever insight, one of the quickest cures is for me to try to work it out in detail. (Admittedly, it doesn't always work: but however many of these you think I have unwittingly smuggled into this book, I can assure you that lots of others have perished in the process of writing it.) But that is only one consideration. A more important one is that this is an indispensable stage of growth. We love to be able to fall back on experts, to believe that we can always be rescued from our bungling by someone who really knows. There is a secret longing in all of us to enlist in Do It Yourself Anonymous, and forswear self-help forever. That will work for your troubles with your carburetor, your leaking roof, even your pinched nerve. But not quite so well for your struggles with *Hamlet,* or with your budget. And as for the problems that touch us most nearly and deeply, there is no escape whatever from taking personal responsibility. When I wonder what I shall do with my life, where

I should pin my hopes, whom I should trust and how I can become wise, there is no entry in the Yellow Pages that can save me. I must find out who and where I am, and choose out of my best semblance of self-possession what ought to follow. And so it is, in a monumentally important way, with Ungifted Christians. They may recognize that their belief is unfinished, their Christianity incomplete, their whole condition, from a traditional point of view, highly eccentric. But they must understand who and where they are, as thoroughly and accurately as they can, before there is much more that can be done. That is one reason why the Ungifted must admit where they stand, explore it, and articulate what it is like to live there. Another reason is for the sake of the Gathering in general: for unless it has the chance to see the Ungifted in the full colors of their spiritual native habitat, it cannot gather them adequately.

I do not mean this negatively. I do not mean that the Ungifted are required simply to declare what it is that they do not yet believe or what does not yet seem to make good sense. That too they must do, but only to set some of the boundaries of the land they live in. The major task is exploring the inside of that land—to be able to find and assert what it is they do believe, however it may or may not square with what they hope to or are told they ought to believe; and to be able to bear joyful witness to what does make sense, without needless anxiety about what doesn't; and to value the creativity of their hope and love as much as it deserves to be valued, without apology. From an orthodox perspective, they are eccentric—off the center. But they have centers of their own. And there is no need to be either apologetic or ashamed about the axis of one's own integrity. It is the main locus of grace for each of us. It is not simply to be admitted: it is to be celebrated. You are not yet a closed question this side of death (and perhaps on the other

163

too), but as long as that is carefully remembered, to rejoice in the excellencies of your eccentricity is to give glory to God.

To take grateful stock of what God hath wrought in you, in his own whimsical way, is one justification for being reflectively forthright about the way of Ungiftedness. The second justification is no less important and no less reverent. The Ungifted show in their lives new ways in which Christianity has turned to bone and spirit. Each of them is a new experiment in Christianity, a new way in which the stuff of living experience is gathered to Christian use and Christian meaning. They are, in short, an important part of the way the Gathering experiments and discovers and grows, lives out its hope.

Christian life is never over, never fully achieved. Every new Christian generation discovers, through the unfolding of new time and new possibilities, new dimensions of Christian experience. It has been so from the beginning. Let me remind you of one of the earliest ways in which the experimentation worked.

In the time of Jesus, the synagogues throughout the world had not only given Jews a diversified home from Europe to Asia: they had made it possible for non-Jews to glimpse what many of them found to be a more profound and worthy form of religion than they had inherited from their own culture. Many of the Gentiles became—not quite converts, but fellow-travelers. They attached themselves to the worshiping synagogues and to the Jewish communities; and although not ready to take the definitive steps of conversion, such as circumcision and the observance of the Jewish dietary laws, they honored the Jewish understanding of God and meditated upon the Jewish scriptures. The Jews even had a name for them, a very respectful name which recognized the deep seriousness of their religious understanding and the genuine devotion that grew from it: they were called the God-Fearers. They were Jewish catechumens—the Ungifted of the synagogues.

If the arrangement of providence had been to leave them by the wayside, as half-converts who fell short of the mark, they could have disappeared from history without a trace. Some of the more conservatively orthodox Jews hoped it would be so. The ambiguous life of the God-Fearers seemed to them an impossible compromise, like hesitating between Baal and Yahweh. Let them be converted, or let them fall away entirely, lost through the fault of their hesitation. But that was not quite the way it worked out.

Before Judaism began losing interest in making converts (which happened shortly afterward, in the midst of terrible wars, and upheavals in Jewish religious life), a new movement presented itself to the God-Fearers: the one which maintained that the Messiah had come in the person of Jesus of Nazareth, and that a new order had begun. Within the Christian mission were many Jews who thought that Gentiles could enter the Gathering of the new order only by becoming Jews, accepting circumcision, the dietary regulations, the whole of the traditional religious law. At first, it appears, this was the dominant view within the Gathering. The God-Fearers were still excluded, still at most fellow-travelers. But as the Christian mission proceeded, a new realization began to dawn on the leaders of the Gathering. It undoubtedly happened in many ways and in various places, but it is told most dramatically in the story of Cornelius.

Cornelius, a Roman Centurion but a man of prayer, had a most puzzling vision in which he was instructed to send to the city of Joppa for a man who was there lodging with a tanner— one Simon bar Jonah, alias Peter. Not being a man to quarrel with heavenly instruction, however bizarre, he sent to Joppa— where an equally bemused Simon Peter was puzzling over a vision he had just received, instructing him to get in touch with a Centurion named Cornelius. Despite his natural hesitation, as a loyal Jew, to get mixed up with the Gentile occupation troops, Peter dutifully answered the call of authority and went to Cornelius in Caesarea, where he preached the Christian good news to God-Fearing but un-Jewish Cornelius and his equally uncircumcised friends. As if the awkwardness of this situation were not enough for Peter to handle, it was suddenly further complicated by a most amazing phenomenon: as Peter preached, the Holy Spirit fell graciously upon these unreconstructed Gentiles and they burst into a Pentecost of ecstasy and joy. What was poor Peter to do? Unlikely as the whole event seemed, it had happened, on the bedrock of present history. Heaven had spoken. Gentiles though they were, Peter accepted them into the Gathering.

It was not altogether easy for Peter to convince the other Jewish Christians that his apparently irregular behavior in baptizing Gentile occupation troops was appropriate and responsible. Some were still inclined to insist that even the most devout of God-Fearers must necessarily become full Jews before they could properly be received into the Gathering. Some were in fact extremely slow to be convinced, and in the ensuing struggle, the Gathering was torn from within more painfully than persecution had ever torn it from without. But the corner had been irrevocably turned, and as the Christian mission spread through the synagogues of Syria and Asia Minor, it carried the news that the work of Christ had put an end to circumcision and dietary law and the need to be children of Abraham's blood and covenant. Some of the Jews in those provincial synagogues generously welcomed this; many others found it a threat and an infidelity to proclaim that what they had known as the holy will of God no longer mattered. But among the first to grasp and celebrate this good news in synagogues throughout the world of the early Christian missions were the God-Fearers. They were home at last. And there, among the Gentile Ungifted of the synagogues, Christianity definitively arrived at a new self-knowledge: the Gathering was no longer a Jewish movement, but a new creation, in which it no longer mattered whether one were slave or free, man or woman, Jew or Gentile—all were welcome, all were made one in Christ. Christianity was finally ready to begin gathering the world.

It was through Cornelius that Peter learned what a series of heaven-sent visions had been unable to teach him. It was through Cornelius and those like him, the Ungifted Gentile God-Fearers, that the Gathering learned that it was no longer bound to its Jewish ancestry. The new generation of Christians learned what the original members, for all their devoted faith, had been unable to discover on their own—new forms of fidelity, new dimensions of Christian experience, a new unfolding of the hidden riches of the Way, the Truth, and the Life to which they had all been called. This was not learned without pain. But despite the mutual doubt and suspicion that inevitably poured in when the walls of uniformity were broken, the right hand of fellowship won out. The unity of the Gathering endured, and established forever a profound lesson: when the time comes for something to be learned or unlearned, it is not through those who cling faithfully to the old limits that this may be done, but only through those to whom the old limits are not convincing.

The unconvinced, the Ungifted, must always at first seem highly suspicious to the Faithed. There is no calculus by which we may distinguish the dawning of a new authentic understanding, or the transformation of a legitimate hope into a novel truth, from sheer infidelity. No calculus; but there is, at least, the human capacity to recognize good news—and even beyond that, there is the ability to perceive in another an integrity that deserves respect and a sense of direction that makes him seem to be on to something important. That at least can bring us to watch and wait, holding our differences in trust within the unity of the Gathering until a judgment greater than yours or mine can make itself felt and known.

I think now of another painful lesson which early Christianity had to learn. As I mentioned earlier, the first generation of Christians seem to have been virtually unanimous in expecting that it would be within their lifetimes that Jesus would return in glory to judge the world. Rightly or wrongly, it was remembered that he had promised one of his audiences that some of them would still be living when it happened. Paul's sense of urgency was fed by this conviction: he assured the Thessalonians that he himself and others who were still alive would be transformed in an instant when the time came, and would join with the resurrected in the eternal kingdom. As the first generation grew old and gradually died away, the belief was kept alive along with the few survivors. The Second Epistle of Peter, perhaps the latest work in the New Testament, is still struggling with the problem of the delay, and promising action. But it was not to be. Eventually, the truth became too obvious to doubt. They had been wrong.

Who were the first to become disconvinced? The records do not reveal it, but it is easy enough to reconstruct what must have happened. The first doubters were certainly thought by the others to be men of little faith—and so it must have been, with some of them: some were only weak, lacking the daring to trust in or even hope for the rapid return of the Son of Man. And so the believers, in their discouragement, wondered whether, when he comes, he will find any faith left on the earth. But there must have been others who were not weak but simply Ungifted in this respect, knowing what the Faithed were claiming but unable to see either that it was true or that it was important enough to deserve their longing.

They were right. They could not yet know that they were

right; it was not as if they were as sure as Faith that he would not come so soon, but merely that they lacked the conviction that he would. And so they must have set about rethinking what it was to live out a Christianity that was not going to be rescued quite so quickly, coming to terms with the consequences of their own Ungiftedness. And as history slowly revealed that this form of Ungiftedness was better adapted to reality than the faith of their opponents, it must have been they, the Ungifted, who taught the rest of the Gathering how to understand what had not happened, and what the Christian Way was to be as a result. They had been right in their unbelief, and in an obscure way, protected from rejection only by the unity of mutual trust, they had been the pioneers of a new Christian self-understanding in which others now needed to share.

It could not have been a painless process. It has never been so; it is not now. Nor should it be: the stakes are too high and the dangers too serious to justify an easy tolerance or a reduction of tension to cozy mutual respect. The Gathering has always contained the weak, the flighty, the unstable, whose doubts and disappointments are dangerously unsettling to the steadiness of the whole community—and it is not always possible to distinguish from them those sounder forms of Ungiftedness through which the truth is destined to be further revealed. The Gathering has always contained members whose indiscriminating faddishness is all too ready to reroute the Way down some ephemeral dead end which history makes momentarily and temptingly available—and who is wise enough to be able always to tell these from the Ungifted visionaries who have really apprehended that the Gathering is being offered by a new time something that will permanently enrich its life? There is no calculus that will solve the problem, just as there is no infallible way of telling the true Faithed from the indiscriminating reactionaries (which, like the poor, the Gathering hath always with them) who are too starkly inhospitable to news of any kind to bother coming to terms with it even when it is good.

How then shall the truth prevail? Not by fiat, or by fad, for neither of these can tell it from its counterfeits. There is finally, I think, one way only. It must be tested by being lived out. Experience is experiment; and until the results of an insight of hope or of love or of belief are registered in the lives of those who found themselves summoned to obey it, and apprehended by those who did not follow, through their affirming participation in the integrity of those who did, there can be no settled verdict. There is no need to hurry. Such things take time; sometimes generations. No matter. The unity of the Gathering is stronger than disagreement, vaster than the generations of Christians through whom it is explored and developed. It can afford all the experimentation to which both the Faithed and the Ungifted understand themselves to be called, and can learn how to live with it, and through it. And through its patient and participating discernment of all the spirits which thus offer themselves to the fulfillment of its life, the Gathering can eventually discover what belongs to Christ.

It is only by this process that the Gathering can come to know itself; it is only by the same process that it can come to know the Christ in whom it believes and whose name it bears, for the Gathering is his body in enduring history—the continuing manifestation among men of the Lord whose life and purpose are disclosed in the developing life and purpose of his Gathering, and in the hopes and beliefs that are born and matured through that life. Unfinished, incomplete, the Gathering goes on about its Father's business—but always in the process of learning what that business is, as it peers through a glass, darkly. It is and is not what it was, and what it once seemed to be. We do not know what it shall become. We do not know what must be learned and what must be unlearned as the Gathering grows, not in age alone but in wisdom and in grace. It may well be that in time more of the traditional beliefs will be honorably surrendered, and transformed into honored memories, as the Gathering once gave up its confidence in an early return of the Lord of Judgment. It may be that new convictions will arise, as there once grew up a confidence that this was a Gathering of Gentiles as well as of Jews. Having once learned that it could not put up with slavery, the Gathering may yet learn that it cannot tolerate war; if it was able to come to terms with the taking of interest on loans, it may even be able to live with the idea of married Cardinals (perish the thought!), or euthanasia, or come to take the problem of poverty more seriously than the problem of heresy. All of this waits to be discovered, by being lived out earnestly and reflectively according to the best lights of all, with a patient mutuality of participation that transcends and embraces all painful differences—but with a faithful tenacity that makes the differences painful.

But in all of this, the affirmation is everything. Nothing must be forgotten, nothing treated with contempt. Nothing once energized by belief or hope or love may be surrendered lightly; what cannot honestly be accepted must at least be understood and honored; and what can no longer be honored must at least be forgiven. For after its love of God, the greatest public secret of the Gathering—which it is still trying to learn and live up to —is its love of men, and of what they have cared for. There is no one so benighted or silly or wicked that the Gathering cannot find a way to cherish him and the story of his days—even to learn from him, though the lesson may be one of tears. That is why the Gathering, when it lives according to its divine command, can trust what it comes to know. It understands with the participating minds of all men, because nothing less will do as a basis for discerning spirits. And that is why in its projects and its hopes it can be about its Father's business; it lives with a life that is born in prayer and nourished by the reverent appropriation of all that men have ever tried to be before the face of the Lord, affirming and reconciling all, everywhere and at every time. This is not tolerance, or forbearance. It is a daring in hope and love and trust that is beyond all reduction and compromise. Only the Gathering could be so audacious as to attempt that; because the Gathering, trying to realize its invitation to divine sonship, strives to be the incarnate echo of the Creator's love for creation.

"When the Son of Man comes, will he find faith on the earth?" The question loses its sting. It may be that the gift of Faith is only for one phase of the Gathering's history. It may indeed come to pass that this gift will be withdrawn from living men. If that should be, the Gathering will continue to remember the faith that once was, and to draw strength from its having been. But its fidelity and its hope are not dependent on the persistence of the Faithed, however much they may be enriched by the Faithed as long as they are with us. Christianity has always been at least a wisdom. This, rather than faith, may be the form in which it is destined to grow into its future. If so, as it grows in age and grace, it may yet gather the world enough to become wisdom itself—Wisdom Himself, the incarnate Word and Love of God. And if this is what the Son of Man finds when he comes, will he be disappointed?

So when we are told that "He is in the desert" and "He is in the secret chambers," or "He is in the Old Way" or "He is in the New Way," we must say both no and yes. These are glimpses of the truth, but we cannot trust in the finality of any of them. All the same, we must attend seriously to each of them and participate with hopeful love in those who live them out, because this is the Way. Each of us, come home from his unvisited Carmel, may finally discover that this is where we are to be visited after all—not spectacularly, but in the quiet of home, where we really have lived all along. And when the Son of Man comes, it may well be that he will find that Christianity has grown up to be the Gathering of the Ungifted.

Epilogue

"*You're almost fifteen minutes late,*" sniffed Jezebel.

"*Sorry,*" said Ahab. "*I got held up.*"

"*And I bet I know with who,*" said Jezebel.

"*Whom,*" said Ahab.

"*Anyway,*" said Jezebel, "*it doesn't matter. I'm not going to the services anyway. I've been thinking over what you said, and I've decided that it's beside the point whether or not I've out-grown those old vacations in the mountains. It's my adult side that I want to develop. And I don't see that the prophets of Baal really have much to do with that—or that tiresome Elijah, either.*"

"*You're the only one who can tell about that,*" said Ahab, "*but speak for yourself. Tiresome as he is, Elijah really gets through to me. I mean, where I am right now. So does the whole Yahwist thing—the prayers, the festivals, the laws even . . .*"

"*Security blanket,*" sniffed Jezebel. "*The lost childhood in the mountains.*"

"*I never had one,*" said Ahab. "*We used to spend the summer in Transjordan, and I'm not very nostalgic about it.*"

"*Small wonder,*" said Jezebel. "*That part of the country is as dry and boring as Yahweh-worship.*"

"*There you go again,*" said Ahab, "*sounding off when you don't know any more about either of them than you could en-grave on a gallstone.*"

175

"Deserts," said Jezebel. "Both of them. I know a desert when I see one."

"That's where you're wrong," said Ahab. "Transjordan is very lush. But I used to visit the desert from there, and I know something about it. Which is more than I can say for you."

"Sand," said Jezebel. "What more is there to it? I know sand when I see it."

"On the surface, yes," said Ahab. "But believe it or not, there are seeds down under there. They survive. They have to. The desert goes sometimes thirty years without rain."

"That's my point," said Jezebel. "So what difference does it make? Dry sand, dry seeds, it's all the same."

"Wrong again," said Ahab. "They survive, waiting for the rain. It happened in our area once, about twenty years ago. A huge cloudburst. Washed out everything down the old creek-beds. After that everything looked normal again. But it had got to the seeds. A while later, all of a sudden, they broke loose and bloomed. All over the desert, where there had seemed to be nothing but sand for as long as almost anyone could remember, they bloomed everywhere: grasses and shrubs and flowers. It was fantastic. Only once every twenty, thirty years. But the seeds are always there, waiting."